RACEWALKING

RACEWALKING

by William Finley and
Marion Weinstein

Photographs by
Sylvia Weinstein

THE STEPHEN GREENE PRESS

LEXINGTON, MASSACHUSETTS

First published in 1985 by The Stephen Greene Press, Inc.
Published simultaneously in Canada by
Penguin Books Canada Limited
Distributed by Viking Penguin Inc., 40 West 23rd Street,
New York, New York 10010

LIBRARY OF CONGRESS CATALOGING IN PUBLICATION DATA
Finley, William, 1944–
   Racewalking.
   Bibliography: p.
   1. Walking (Sports)   I. Weinstein, Marion.   II. Title.
GV1071.F49   1984   796.5'1   84-13812
ISBN 0-8289-0534-7

Printed in the United States of America by
Hamilton Printing Company, Rensselaer, New York
Designed by Irving Perkins Associates

ACKNOWLEDGMENTS

The authors wish to thank:

Susan Weiser Finley and Sylvia Weinstein, for writing and editing help. Richard Curtis, our agent; all the people we interviewed: Richard and Susan Friess Goldman, Nick Bdera, Ron Laird, Henry and Hilde Laskau, Dr. Lawrence J. Cohn, and Dr. Raymond Koval. Andrea Miller and Eileen Greeley for typing. Muffin and Toto for encouragement. Abe Ginsberg for printing photos. Patricia Millman for research. Ellen Goldman for advice. Naomi Bernstein, F.Y.I.: research. Ralph and Anna Shapiro for posing.

Author's Note

With this or any other program of exercise, it is advised that you consult your physician first. In the case of racewalking, it is entirely possible that your physician will want to join you.

—W. F. and M. W.

CONTENTS

"I started racewalking primarily because of my running injuries. And I started to like the feeling of racewalking for a number of reasons—one of which was being able to racewalk when I couldn't run— because running hurt and racewalking didn't hurt. I was also able to keep my aerobic endurance up, to stay aerobically fit. And I was also able to exercise my upper body; this is what racewalking does for you and running does not. So as I look now at the entire picture, it really doesn't make sense to run. You can get all the benefits of running without the injuries of running. And not only all the benefits, but more benefits, because racewalking is more of a total body fitness exercise than running is . . . . My first marathon, I probably beat about 2,500 runners."

—RICHARD GOLDMAN,
CHAMPION RACEWALKER
AND FOUNDER
OF THE METROPOLITAN
RACEWALKERS

Richard Goldman.

INTRODUCTION

"I often see injured runners with shin splints, fatigue fractures, bone spurs, ligamentous injuries, toe destruction and other foot problems, bursitis and tendonitis . . . I think that racewalking is much safer. It's a much healthier activity. One does not stress the muscular-skeletal system to the same extent and can get the same benefit out of it; and it can fit the needs of a larger population."

—RAYMOND KOVAL, M.D.,
ORTHOPEDIC SURGEON

Racewalking as an effective form of exercise is almost astonishing in its simplicity: *walking* —and making positive use of the body's internal rhythms. What could be more natural? Often in our search for new disciplines or techniques to improve mind and body we tend to overlook a most basic activity—one that exists, so to speak, right in our own backyard.

This simple activity is walking. When done in the most basic way—and you've been doing it essentially all along—it holds enormous potential for transformation of psyche and physique. The result? New levels of energy, health, and attractiveness.

First let us point out that racewalking is not merely "walking" exactly as you may have experienced it in the past:

- paying little or no attention to posture or pace
- carrying bags/packages/groceries/umbrellas, etc.
- wearing restrictive clothing and shoes

- paying more attention to *where* you're going than how you're getting there.

In contrast, racewalking is an experience which involves:

- following a specific course and distance
- paying careful attention to form—internal as well as external
- wearing your most comfortable clothing, and running shoes
- paying careful attention to *how* you'll get to where you're *really* going: your state of being.

Racewalking is a time-honored sport which emphasizes a heightened awareness of integral physical detail: synchronized movement of arms and legs and specifically designed harmonious motions of the upper and lower portions of the body. Racewalking takes some concentration at first, before it becomes gloriously automatic. But it is easily within the grasp of anyone who can walk—and within a short period of time.

If You Can Walk, You Can Racewalk

You don't have to be or try to be an athlete, jock, stoic, or fanatic. You need no special instructors, gym, equipment, weights, outfits, health clubs—nothing other than a good pair of shoes, comfortable clothing, and this book. Racewalking doesn't cost anything. You can do it anywhere. No advanced state of physical fitness is required in order to begin. You can be overweight, underweight, old, young, or middle-aged. You can even be what is sneeringly referred to by those perspiration-drenched, Perrier-guzzling, bronzed, spongecake athletes as *out-of-shape.*

Racewalking is, in fact, an easy way to get yourself in shape and stay that way simply by pursuing it consistently with no goals other than fitness and fun. For beginners, the goal is not necessarily speed or distance. The goal is to allow yourself to feel as good as you potentially can feel. Perhaps you have had glimpses of this good feeling already: dancing at a party, performing some other sport you can already accomplish, or even taking a brisk walk outdoors. Or perhaps you *remember* feeling this good when you were younger than you are now. . . .

Go for the Gold

Beyond fitness and fun, the higher levels of racewalking offer a vast new field just waiting for its first heroes and heroines to pave the way. There are racewalkers in training right now who have gone from being mediocre joggers to gold medal racewalking champions in two to three years. For those runners who are tired of the New York Marathon/Boston Marathon stampeding, lemming-like hordes, there awaits the unique thrill of being in the vanguard of a newly discovered sport. New records are waiting to be set. The Olympics beckon.

The Hidden Gift of Racewalking

Energy: We all have the potential to perceive and use energy because it is already within us. The process of racewalking helps us to release the natural energy flow, tapping a universal source. Instead of straining to create physical stamina we use the internal strength that *already exists.* We unleash energy, we let it happen, we do not fake it. Our own energy simply reveals itself to us by acting for us and through us.

The human brain and body have enormous potential which is unacknowledged, unrecognized, and apparently unavailable to most of us in this culture. The culture has conditioned too many of us to think that we have to work to "build" energy . . . to pay a fortune for it . . . to sweat and strain to "create" a thinner, healthier, and stronger body . . . to perhaps even employ artifice, to "make" ourselves look younger and more attractive. . . and generally to superimpose some penalty, system, or discipline to change ourselves. These are unnecessary limitations. They deny the value and inherent beauty and power of who and what we already are.

In racewalking, we choose to accept ourselves *exactly as we are* as a starting point. We each can allow ourselves to develop more fully to our own optimum state—rather than a facsimile of someone else's ideal.

There is nothing frivolous about wanting to look and feel our best. These are healthy desires for everyone. And there is nothing lazy about wanting a fitness regime which is painless, simple, and easy. And fast. Why not?

Just walk along with us. . . .

RACEWALKING

CHAPTER 1

MEET THE AUTHORS

Little did we know we'd ever be writing a book such as this one. True, we are writers; true, we both have been known to walk and have, in fact, been doing so since the age of (approximately) one. But we must confess right at the start that we have never been what could be remotely considered athletes. We always thought that athletes were special, comprising a particular subdivision of the human race, a category which some people were born into and others could enter into—if they were lucky—after years of intense training, straining, and effort which precluded just about anything else in life.

Being non-athletes by birth, temperament, physique, and inclination, we naturally admired and envied anyone whose body was firmer, stronger, more graceful, or younger-looking than ours. After all, such base envy is the American way. So, upon reaching adulthood, we immediately set about trying to change ourselves. Over the past 15 years we have tried (individually and together): gymnastics, yoga, jogging, running, modern dance, tap-dancing, swimming, aerobics, isometrics, calesthenics, tennis, Royal Canadian Air Force Exercises, diets, fasting, massage, saunas, steambaths, exercise machines, health clubs, stretching, and hanging from a trapeze to the derisive laughter of two bored Latvian gymnasts. You can't say we didn't try.

And we did pretty well, too. William displayed a spider-like agility in the film "The

Phantom of The Paradise," Brian DePalma's rock 'n roll version of "The Phantom of The Opera." In order to fill out his skin-tight black leather outfit, he had to work out with trainer Bill Shephard for two months. Finally, he was able to climb the rafters of the Paradise Theater, run amuck in the villain's office, and actually swing on ropes to rescue sweet Jessica Harper à la Errol Flynn. Running amuck, as horror film buffs know, is not a piece of cake.

Marion, safely ensconsed behind a radio microphone for 14 years, had to overcome intense stage-fright and knocking of knees in order to stand up and do live comedy in front of thousands of people at radio station benefits and in nightclubs. After mastering a series of athletic warmups with trainer Ellen Goldman, she finally graduated to TV talk shows with Tom Snyder and Mike Douglas. And entrances on national television, as video aficionados know, are knee-knockers in the extreme.

Realizing the importance to our work of keeping fit, we both reached the point where we could jog with relative ease for two miles last summer—even though our pace was a bit slower than that of casual strollers who passed us regularly. But after any strenuous activity, each of us always had to stop everything, take a hot shower, and lie down—not always in that order. Sometimes we had to lie down first.

Exercise which cuts into one's life so completely can prove discouraging as a daily regime. How can you go running if you have an appointment with your agent later in the day? You can't lie down in an agent's office . . . and you certainly cannot nap while taking a meeting with a tinseltown mogul . . . or snooze in a publisher's inner sanctum. How can you catch a train, plane, or taxi if you're too exhausted and aching to move your feet? How can you cook dinner, eat dinner, meet friends, watch television—never mind sit at the typewriter and work—if your brain is befogged (and befuddled) with fatigue? These were questions we strove to answer.

Above William's Manhattan apartment lived advertising photographer Richard Goldman, a strapping physical specimen with the body of a middleweight and an outrageously cheerful disposition. He was a racewalker, and one day he took William on an excursion in Washington Square Park. But wait, we'll let William tell you how it all came about.

mered bravely. 'Wh . . . wh . . . whenever you want. Let's get together.'

"I figured I'd never hear from *him* again, when lo and behold the very next day the phone rang and he said, 'Meet you at eight-thirty!' I put on my jogging clothes with trepidation. Well, he took me on the same route I'd suffered earlier—down Fifth Avenue and through Washington Square Park—but this time it was an incredibly delightful morning. He taught me the rudiments of racewalking, and I found myself actually able to do it *and* have a good time doing it. I was not tired, feeling dizzy, or out of breath; afterwards, I even went *out on my own* for seven days and found I could easily do three and one-half miles! I also noticed I had cut down on my smoking and had lost three pounds. But the most amazing phenomenon to me was a five-fold increase in energy! I didn't need naps anymore!"

William's Story

"I was run-down from my annual winter bout with the flu. My doctor prescribed jogging, something I felt I could do to a certain extent, having jogged up to two miles the summer before, and having kept it up somewhat over the winter. For company, I decided to start my new regime with a film producer who'd best remain nameless: He took me out for an allegedly healthy, friendly jog in midtown traffic at rush hour. With Washington Square as our destination, he sped ahead of me, taunting and urging me on with the skill of DeSade, until I finally plotzed in humiliated exhaustion.

"In the days following while I was recovering from this, I bumped into my neighbor, Richard Goldman, as usual in his athletic costume, in the elevator. He said, 'Bill, when are you going to try racewalking with me?' I stam-

Marion's Story

"When Bill told me he was racewalking in the park, the first thing that impressed me was the time he went: eight-thirty a.m.! He's always done his jogging and other exercise later in the day—as late as possible, in fact, after he'd gone to all his appointments and done his writing work, so that he'd have the time to lie down afterwards for as long as necessary. When he told me he'd gone the next day and the next my problem was remembering the name of what he was doing. I'd ask him, 'Are you going walk-running today?' or 'Did you go fast-walking?' I couldn't remember what it was called until I tried it.

"He taught me and his wife Susan at the same time. Of course Susan picked it up immediately—she is an athlete and a dancer—but it took me seven sessions until I mastered i

At first I felt very self-conscious, sort of like Mae West sashaying along, swinging my hips. But the amazing part from the very beginning was the speed. I actually found myself moving faster than when I jogged or ran, and I was able to do two miles quite easily.

"After the magical seventh session, I knew I 'had' it because when I got home I didn't collapse on my bed. I felt exhilarated and full of energy, and did heavy work in the garden for several hours. And the best bonus of all is my weight! I have had a weight problem for some time, and in the first week of racewalking I lost four pounds. Now that the book is finished I've lost *25 pounds* and three inches from my hips."

Richard Goldman, who introduced William to racewalking, is of the athletic species, an ex-runner capable of many other physical activities besides racewalking. So you see, this book is not *only* for non-athletes. If you are athletically inclined, you don't have to give up marathon running, weekend soccer, or pumping iron to enjoy and benefit from racewalking. This book is for athletes and non-athletes alike, even though it was written by non-athletes— but wait a minute: thanks to racewalking, we just may be changing our classification.

What Is Racewalking?

Racewalking is essentially a smooth, even, somewhat rapid stride, with shoulders and hips swinging rhythmically. The body is accelerated as if by an invisible engine, yet the motion appears effortless. Because the upper extremities and torso are involved as much as the lower, it becomes apparent that physical advantages exceed the more limited movements of jogging or running—activities to which racewalking is most frequently compared. Unlike jogging and running, racewalking utilizes the muscles of the shoulders, upper arms, and upper back. In women, the pectoral muscles surrounding the breasts are also employed because the upper arms are moving. But there is no harsh up-and-down motion—no jiggling of breasts, no tearing of tissues, no pounding reverberations of head and neck, no strain on feet, legs, or knees. Consequently, racewalking is easier than running, and has no built-in negative side-effects or occupational hazards such as fatigue fractures, tendonitis, or "runner's knee." Breathing is deep, rhythmic, and natural. There is no huffing and puffing and no profuse sweating (although of course some perspiration may occur, depending on the weather). Racewalkers dress the same as most joggers and runners and feel the same pride in their sport. Shorts and tee shirts are worn in summer, sweatsuits in winter. Running shoes and cotton socks are *de rigeur*.

Who Are the Racewalkers?

They are the wounded joggers, disillusioned runners, expectant mothers, people of advanced age, recuperating heart patients, children, dieters, and performers. And *potential* racewalkers include those millions of people who sought the benefits of running and jogging, and found it just too tiring and too hazardous, as well as those 35 million people who walk daily for exercise and need only to make a few adjustments in their approach and style in order to become expert racewalkers.

We are fully aware of a tendency toward evangelical zeal in books on running and body-building, specifically those written by ex-non-exercisers. We know there are claims that running cures all ills whether they be insomnia, indigestion, impotence, depression, obesity, and various cardio-pulmonary troubles.

We don't want to sound like born-again walkers, prophets of yet another spiritually tinged bright-eyed fitness cult. So we will not make any exorbitant claims.
BUT
if after you start racewalking you find yourself: sleeping better . . . enjoying your extra energy flow . . . digesting your food comfortably . . . having a trim, lean body . . . a healthy sex life . . . increased awareness . . . and prone to attacks of cheerfulness and downright optimism. . . .

CHAPTER 2

YOU BEGIN

Today is the day you're going to start race-walking! It's a lovely day, the sun is shining (well, even if it isn't, it's still a wonderful day to begin). The birds are singing and/or the cars are honking.

Put on your shorts. Put on your tee shirt. Slip into your sweatsocks and lace up your running shoes.

If you're going out alone, stride purposefully out the door.

If you're planning on company, call up your friend(s) and say, "See you at our appointed place soon," and then stride purposefully out the door.

Go to your appointed place.

Do your warmups (see the next chapter and Chapter 13).

Now there's nothing left for you to do but start.

To Start

Walk along normally, swinging your arms loosely.

Allow them to swing freely from the shoulder blades.

The key is to *pay attention* to what your body *is* doing, instead of forcing it to do anything or being oblivious to your actions.

First notice how your arms swing in opposition to your feet: When your right foot goes out, your left arm goes out. This all happens quite naturally: right, left . . . right, left . . . keep going. . . . You can feel that opposition pulling you forward . . . in a pendulum-like motion . . . the top of the pendulum emanating from the upper center of your spine.

Continue your walk.

Now all you have to do is move your arms slightly faster.

You will become aware (slowly and almost imperceptibly) that as your arms move faster, you increase the natural pendulum movement . . . and you can't help but go slightly faster with your feet!

This is the secret of racewalking: your arms propel you automatically because they make your feet go faster.

The faster the arms, the faster the feet.

You would have to fight your body's instinctive movement in order to prevent this smooth, swinging effect.

Now, increase the speed of your arms . . . a bit more . . .

You will notice the arms are starting to bend at the elbow.

Allow this to continue until they form an "L" shape (see illustration). This is known as THE PISTON or THE PUSHER.

At this point if you tried to make your arms hang in a straight position you would just slow yourself down. The piston effect propels you forward, pushing you ahead.

Now to complete the piston image: form each

The Piston or Pusher.

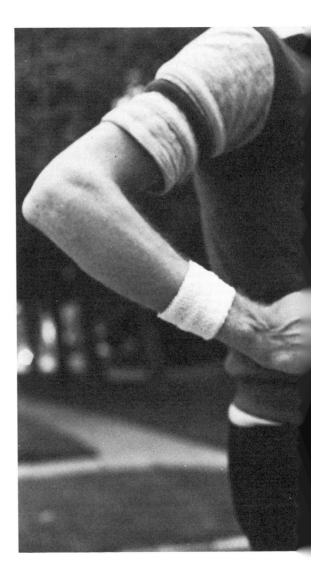

hand into a loose fist. Concentrate, imagining a point in front of your eyes, and swing your fists into it as you go. This may remind some of you of punching—an image some people can relate to easily and others (women, especially) might find a novel experience. Picture the punching bag floating along just ahead of you. Keep on punching, but not too violently.

You are flying.

Continuing at this pace, punching as you go, don't alter anything but slightly increase the effort: You will find yourself moving along with the liberating sensation of gliding. In fact, at this point, if you close your eyes, you could imagine *you are flying!!*

Next, shift your attention to your feet (eyes are open, of course). Leading with the heel,

Congratulations! You're racewalking!

each foot should reach forward into the space in front of you.

As you land on your heel, flex your foot as much as you can. Ninety degrees is the desired angle of foot to leg; however, 45 degrees is fine to start.

As the front of your foot hits the ground, push off with your toes while keeping your leg straight.

. . . Left, right . . . left, right.

Keep going.

. . . CONGRATULATIONS! YOU'RE RACE-WALKING!!!

At this point, you will notice your lower body swaying from side to side. This is the unique racewalking stride.

This heel-to-toe/straight-leg/arms-in-opposition movement produces a rocking motion in the pelvis. So you see why some people feel racewalking is like dancing.

The tango . . . the rhumba. The hips undulate!

Runners and joggers note: This is very different from the up-and-down, bouncing rhythm you are accustomed to. We hope you enjoy it as you ease on down the road.

We realize you've just learned a lot for your first day. IF YOU GET TIRED, or if at any time you feel you have lost the racewalking stride, simply STOP, go back to an ordinary walk, and gradually build up your pace as described above.

At this point, you've racewalked about 20 or 25 minutes, which is about a mile for a beginner, and you (and your friend) should be back at your starting point just about now. You'll be happy to see you're not sweating profusely, you're not out of breath, you're not staggering with exhaustion. A few of you may feel just a trifle pooped—but remember, this is your first day and you have accomplished quite a bit. You have earned a cool drink and a hot shower.

As you're singing and soaping in the shower, you can look forward to the racewalker's reward: After mastering the basics of this sport (which takes approximately seven sessions) you *always* feel better when you finish than you did when starting.

CHAPTER 3

A FEW BEGINNING WARMUPS

Warmup stretches serve two functions: They literally warm you up by getting the blood circulating, and they stretch otherwise "cold" muscles so that you do not risk tearing or pulling them when you start racewalking.

You need a whole spectrum of exercises to warm up the various muscles and joints of your body. We have chosen four warmup stretches to start you off, but we hope you will also study and use the larger group of exercises presented in Chapter 13.

Wall Push

Face a wall (or anything you can push against).

Right leg in front of left.

Right knee bent.

Toes straight ahead.

Both heels on the ground.

Let hips move toward the wall.

Feel the stretch at the back of the extended leg.

Relax into the stretch for ten to twelve seconds.

Alternate—left leg in front.

Good for: calf muscles, Achilles tendons (joining the calf and the heel).

Wall Push.

Hamstring Stretch.

Hamstring Stretch

Rest right foot on object (such as a stool, stair-
step, or fence), leg extended, knee straight.

Toes point straight up, turned slightly inward.

Stretch with arms toward toes. (Note: Many
people cannot touch their toes right away. Do
not force.)
Relax into the stretch for ten to 12 seconds or
until you feel muscles release.

Alternate—left foot on object.

Good for: hamstring, inner and outer thighs,
and back muscles.

The Stork

Hold onto a wall or other support.

Balance on one leg.

Hold other foot by the toe, bending knee.

Careful not to yank or pull too hard.

Pull toe toward your buttock, concentrating on the feeling of stretch in your front leg muscles.

Alternate—other leg.

Good for: strengthening quadriceps (anterior or front thigh muscle), knee stability.

The Stork.

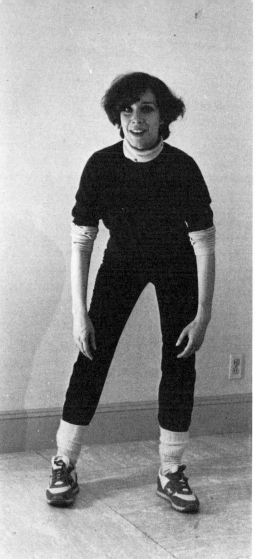

The Hip Roll.

Hip Roll

Legs slightly apart, feet parallel, bent knees.

Relax arms and shoulders.

Let's circle right:

Push hips as far to the right as possible.

Slowly rotate hips clockwise making a large circle.

Move hips from right to back to left to forward, as smoothly as possible.

Keep the motion round, not jerky.

Repeat for six circles.

Reverse direction—six more.

Hint: If you need help, put your hands on your hips and push your hips along the circle.

Good for: flexibility in the hip joint, isolating and loosening the muscles of the pelvic girdle.

Now we hope you're feeling all stretched out and ready to go. (Remember to repeat some warmup exercises when you return—when they will be renamed "warmdown." Some people think that *after* a workout is the most important time of all to stretch.)

Now that you're ready to go, what better place to proceed than learning more about proper racewalking form?

CHAPTER 4

GOOD FORM AND HOW TO GET IT

Now that you've warmed up and understand the basics of racewalking—and we hope you actually have done some of it—the time has come to explore the finer points of form so that you can perfect your style. It's important to do this at the beginning of your racewalking experience; proper technique can then become second nature to you. If you take your time looking into it now, your form will become— if not an actual piece of cake—much easier to deal with. In fact, it's fun to concentrate on each component of one aspect of form each time you go out: For instance, one day arms, one day torso, etc. You will be amazed at how all this falls together into your own best racewalking style.

Get To Know Your Body In Seven Easy Sessions

This chapter may seem a bit complicated in the beginning, but don't let it throw you. This is the chapter you'll be referring to again and again as you become a more proficient racewalker and seek to improve your technique.

Since racewalking is an international sport, it has rules. The rules define the skill and the form. At first glance the rules look easy, but following them—especially when going fast or in competition—might seem difficult. With time and practice, however, you can use them to your advantage, especially while working on your technique. Here are the rules:

1. Contact with the ground must be maintained.
2. The advancing foot must make contact with the ground before the rear foot leaves the ground.
3. And last (to quote the Rulebook of the International Athlete Federation, the IAAF): "During the period of each step in which a foot is on the ground, the leg shall be straightened (i.e., not bent at the knee) at least for one moment."

These rules seem to be designed to keep racewalkers from lapsing into running. Our seven sessions will keep you within the rules while maintaining easy movement and an enjoyable pace. Six of the sessions deal with isolating one particular area of the body each time you racewalk. And the seventh gives you an opportunity to combine them.

The areas of the body on which we shall be concentrating are pelvis/hips, torso, legs, arms, feet, and head. Then we shall combine them all.

The goal, while working with each of these, is to concentrate on each area and to relax into the natural use of each muscle group, rather than trying to push or force an effect. Of course, the best way to work on these muscles is to concentrate on them *while* we are moving them.

Also, please bear in mind that the warmups recommended in the previous chapter and in Chapter 13 are designed to limber up all of these areas. It is important to do at least some of the warmups before each racewalking session.

Now, let's start with the pelvis, because this area is the center of motion for the racewalker.

The Pelvis/Hips—Session 1

First of all, what do we mean by *pelvis*? Elvis knew, of course, and he would have been a terrific racewalker. If you can remember his gyrations, then you already know the basics of properly initiated movement in the pelvis.

The pelvic region means the area starting with the groin and wrapping around the hips to the buttocks. It is actually the body's center of gravity, and the place from which the body moves.

THE "HEAVY WALKER"

Have you ever seen a walker or runner whose feet hit the ground with a thud, with each step? The person may not necessarily be heavy or elderly, but somehow he or she still seems heavy and earthbound.

THE "BOUNCY WALKER"

Or, have you seen a runner or walker whose heels seem never to touch the ground, who simply bounces along on the balls of the feet? Such a person moves more up and down than forward.

The heavy walker's weight seems to be held in the knees and feet. The bouncy walker seems to lift and tense from the upper torso. Neither of these methods is suitable for racewalking as both create unnecessary tensions in the body.

The most effective way to move forward is by supporting the weight in the pelvic region. As mentioned above, some of the warmup exercises are designed to help you locate and isolate the feeling of using this area. If you can't locate it, you can't feel it.

Have you warmed up? Good. Now, let's get up on our feet and see what the hip/pelvis area does when we are walking normally. First, walk about slowly and notice that as you walk your front foot pulls you and your back foot pushes you. To put it another way: your front foot prevents you from losing your balance entirely, and your back foot and leg propel you forward. Walking has been defined as "the prevention of falling." In fact, technically you *do* start to fall forward each time you take a step. It is the automatic weight shift that counteracts the possibility of actually falling down.

Walk slowly, but not flat-footed or sliding along like an ice-skater. Increase the distance between your feet (the length of your stride) and keep walking slowly. Remember taking "giant steps" in *Simon Says*?

May I?

Yes, you may. So, take a giant step. Let's say your left leg is your supporting leg, as you start out. Your pelvis is over your left leg. As the right leg moves from behind, out of the pull/push: (1) the hip moves forward, and (2) the pelvis is lifted off the supporting leg, and suspended momentarily between your two legs. Then, as you move onto your right leg, your new supporting leg, the pelvis moves up and over *that* leg so that it's directly on top of the right leg. If you could trace the path of your pelvis in space, it would create a slight "U."

By taking these giant steps, we have discovered how the pelvic area lifts and moves our weight *forward* through space. We hope you have discovered this, too.

Now let's apply these normal walking principles to the art of racewalking.

he place from which the body moves—the pelvis.

One basic racewalking idea is to *support, lift,* and *drop* from the pelvis: lifting the back leg up and over the support leg in order to give it the opportunity to straighten into the forward-thrusting heel. Each time you move forward from one leg to another, you are shifting and lifting your body's weight. Each of these shifts in weight is on a slightly horizontal plane as you shift from the right leg to the left leg to the right leg, and so on.

But the basic motion is from front to back. (Note: The Pelvic Shuffle exercise in Chapter 13 duplicates the rocking experience of this motion.) As the right leg swings front, the right side of the pelvis (the right hip) slides on a horizontal plane to the *outside, forward,* and *down.* This happens in an instant. It gives racewalking that unique hip swivel which actors like Dan Ackroyd and Peter Sellers have immortalized on film. But for us, the important part is the internal sensation of the *hip leading the impulse* of the stride.

To help connect with this sensation, here's a powerful image which Eric Hawkins, the great choreographer, dancer, and movement expert, shares with his students: Think of the area at the front of your hips as being two car headlights. Now, as you're walking, think of these headlights as moving smoothly forward in space. Or as Ellen Goldman, another wonderful dancer and movement teacher, would say, "Send your hips *ahead* of you." Another useful image would be to picture yourself being pulled evenly forward by a magnetic force which is far ahead in the distance, connected with your pelvic center.

All of this is a roundabout way of saying that good racewalking technique is always an extension of your own natural movement. Rather than adding extra movement, the object is to reduce movement to simple basics in order to discover the most effective way to go from point A to point B while walking fast.

During the racewalking session in which you decide to concentrate on pelvis and hips, keep this in mind: *Forward, up, and over!* (in the pelvic area) each time you are shifting your weight onto a new supporting leg. (1) *Forward* is a directional thrust to add inches to each stride, (2) *Up and over* is a slight internal motion, and (3) Also note: an inch or two in the hips translates to a reach of four to six inches further with your feet!

Keep the pelvic motion fluid. Rotation is from front to back, not side to side. Every time you take a step, think *forward, up, and over,* in the pelvic area. Got it? And as you keep thinking *forward, up, and over,* try to relax about it. Don't bounce up and down, and don't forget to breathe.

The Torso—Session II

The torso evolves from the latin "Thyrsus," meaning a stalk or stem. And that's what it is: the vertical column of the body. It's also defined as the body's trunk and it's packed with important items: the heart, the lungs, the diaphragm, the ribs, and the digestive system. And that's a lot of weight (not to mention the head, neck, and arms which are supported from it). In racewalking, what's important is that the torso sits on the pelvis and swivels from side to side. If the torso is considered a trunk, like a tree, then the arms could be viewed as branches.

Venus de Milo is, perhaps, the most famous torso in the world; in classical sculpture, the ideal torso was considered a focal point of beauty. We're not saying that people will ask you to pose for statues, but your torso will improve from racewalking because it gets such a healthy, muscle-toning workout every time you take a step.

If you have followed our suggestions in the first session and are beginning to develop the feeling of lifting from the pelvis, your next jo is to relax the torso. In this way the torso can respond more readily to the impulses coming from the pelvis. You will find yourself breathing much more easily, and you'll be walking tall.

You also will notice that your relaxed torso responds to the opposition between your arms and legs, that all-important feature of racewalking. Lots of people have an image of the arms "starting" at the shoulders; instead, try to imagine that the arms' movement is initiated in the torso, from the center of the spine. If the torso is relaxed the arms are less likely to be tight, and vice versa. Your arm swing will have more power.

When told to "stand up straight" most people will immediately suck in their stomachs, throw back their shoulders, push out their rib cage—and stop breathing. They stop breathing because they've become so rigid. No wonder

The Ultimate Torso.

most of us don't "stand straight" most of the time! It's totally exhausting: The result, no doubt, of too many World War II movies with the troops being inspected by John Wayne. So, if you're tempted to stand like this, please keep in mind that *you are not really standing straight*. You are probably hyper-extending—arching—your ribs and your back. And also remember that John Wayne isn't going to come and inspect you. You don't have to stand "at attention" to stand straight!

Most people (yes, even we!) don't have perfect posture. Oh, most of us had perfect posture when we were babies, but then various things happened to us and we started stooping, straining, leaning, lurching, and otherwise developing our postural personalities. (Most often the problems come subliminally in adolescence, such as the feeling of being too tall, too fat, too shy, or too whatever. Poor posture becomes a nearly permanent overcompensation for such feelings of insecurity.)

People who walk about in a perpetual state of imbalance are, in effect, allowing their own body weight to crush them (as perhaps they feel that life is caving in on them). And while we are not writing a book about body language here (although we have studied this fascinating subject), it's important to be aware that poor posture telegraphs a whole variety of subliminal messages to other people in daily encounters. So, it is not an exaggeration to say that a whole spectrum of social and professional dealings can automatically improve simply by having a posture that telegraphs confidence and good health.

Be patient. Be aware that your present posture is probably the result of years of physical and emotional habits. You might even be psychologically attached to it. So poor posture cannot be expected to change overnight. But it can change, simply by following the guidelines in this chapter (one of the wonderful side benefits of racewalking).

Regarding posture in general and racewalking specifically, it might be a good idea to have a friend monitor you from time to time; you can't always tell what's good posture from the *inside*. At first good posture often feels wrong, like leaning too far back or forward, simply because you are not used to standing correctly.

An image can be very helpful.

Think of your pelvis as a platter. Does that sound too odd? Trust us. To extend the image, think of your torso as sitting on the platter. And your legs are the waiter carrying the platter along.

With our theater background, we have found it very helpful to work with images. If someone tells you what to do from the outside in ("put your stomach there, put your neck *there*"), you may end up in a pretzel-like pose. But if you work from the inside *out*, all your parts will be in their most natural placement. Try this handy platter image when you go out for this session. We think you'll see what we mean.

But wait. Don't go out the door just yet. To make the image even clearer, we have a warm-up exercise to help you perceive how your spine works to hold your torso in place. Let's face it, without your spine, your torso would be going nowhere. Sure, there are animals who don't have spines . . . but they don't racewalk. They undulate. (And usually underwater.)

Ready?

Spine Rollup

Stand with legs slightly apart, knees slightly bent. Bend forward from your buttocks, so that everything above them (torso, arms, shoulders head) is hanging down toward the floor. Leaving everything else relaxed, use the pelvic groin area to lift *slowly* and place one vertebra over the other like building blocks.

As the upper vertebrae move into place, you'll notice how the shoulders relax and drop down. Then the vertebrae in the neck place the head in correct alignment above them. Think of the top of your head as a helium balloon floating up to the ceiling . . . and now you are standing truly straight. Try it while moving.

The spinal lift will enable you to keep erect while racewalking without stiffening, hunching, or losing your balance. It will also help you breathe from the diaphragm. (For more about this exercise see Chapter 13.)

And speaking of breathing: There's a lot more space for air in you than you probably knew about (or even suspected). Why? Because when your upper body is erect and relaxed, you are giving your lungs and diaphragm room to breathe.

The lungs themselves are not muscles: they are elastic sacs—vessels for containing air and extracting oxygen from that air. The expansion and contraction (pull in, push out) you feel when you breathe comes from the muscles connecting with the ribs' chest wall and diaphragm. You can't increase the amount of oxygen your lungs extract (about 20 percent) from the air, but you can increase the amount of air coming in. How? By altering your perception of where the air goes when you breathe it in—not by just using the upper chest, but almost the entire torso.

Try this for yourself:

Lie on the floor on your back, knees bent, legs slightly apart, sides of feet parallel on the floor. Try to relax the small of your back into the floor, and relax your rib cage.

Lengthen the back of your neck against the floor and relax your jaw. Now, slowly inhale, and as you do so think of allowing the air to fill up, not just your lungs, but your entire *back*

from the pelvis up to your shoulders; and your entire front, from your lower abdomen all the way up to the throat. Think of every empty space in the torso filling with air. Now, hold a moment, then s-l-o-w-l-y exhale until all the air is out. Repeat.

Many people as a result of tension and habit are shallow breathers, and tend to breathe from the rib cage up. Now that you have experienced how much room for air really exists in your torso, try to breathe from as low in the torso as possible while standing. Coaches and athletes call this "sucking wind" and "belly breathing." Both terms are helpful but a bit misleading, because you should also remember your back has space. The object is not to fill your stomach with air (you could develop "the burps"), but to use the elasticity of the diaphragm to pull air first to the bottom of the torso, then the back, and then the top, allowing cool air to fill up the vessel like water filling up a well.

The combination of an erect, relaxed torso with this deep breathing allows the lungs to open up, making each inhalation an exhilarating experience. As you continue your racewalking sessions and develop your speed or distance, you will find that a greater capacity for oxygen consumption will increase your endurance and stamina.

And now a word about "aerobic": a trendy label, but exactly what does it mean? Just what we said above: it is a measure of the body's ability to take in, extract, and utilize oxygen. As the oxygen goes into the bloodstream, it slows down the heartbeat of the body at rest. And this *prolongs life*.

Any activity can be aerobic in effect if it is rhythmic and repetitive and at peak output. Vigorous dancing in a gym could be considered aerobic, as could swimming. Marathon running, however, is acknowledged worldwide as a leading source of aerobic fitness. Now, what about racewalking? Recent studies have proved that competitive racewalkers are equal in fitness with highly trained marathon runners—specifically in lungs and heart.[1] In fact, a government-funded group of sports medicine specialists concluded:

> Physiological and selected psychological characteristics of nine highly trained racewalkers were studied and the results compared to those for distance runners and other athletes of similar age . . . the physiological and psychological profile of the racewalker is indeed similar to that of the marathon runner.[2]

The Legs—Session III

The legs provide the distinctive signature movement of racewalking form. With runners, the legs execute a series of leaps with brief moments when both feet are off the ground. As you may remember from the rules we quoted above, in racewalking you don't leave the ground with one foot until the other foot is firmly on the ground, at which time the leg above is straight (with its knee locked).

Like everything else in racewalking, these rules may seem arbitrary at first. But as you start to get the feel of the sport, you will see that this technique provides you with the longest and strongest stride.

Because you will be lifting your body weight from the pelvis, and because you are not subjected to the continual pounding of the runner's leaps, racewalking avoids potential damage to the parts of the body which runners may sustain. With every leap, a runner propels his/her body into the air, so that the landing foot and leg must cushion three to four times the body's weight. This ceaseless pounding can

eventually take its toll on the foot, knee, leg, groin, and lower back. Because the racewalker has both feet on the ground for as long as possible (if only for a fraction of a second), and at least one foot on the ground at all times, racewalking provides a more fluid and less jarring shift in body weight. (For this reason, racewalking has been discovered as ideal training for runners and other sportspeople—especially those who have been injured.)

"Indeed, racewalking is a safe refuge for any injured athlete. It is the perfect sport for recuperating from some other sport. . . the ailing athlete who turns to racewalking will soon find himself on the mend."[3]

The runner who switches to racewalking for its therapeutic effect will discover other assets of the sport he might not have suspected, such as a sure way to physical fitness. Work done by Dr. Michael Pollock at Wake Forest University has shown that it makes little difference on the cardiovascular fitness meter as to whether you run or walk. When intensity, frequency, and duration are similar, results are similar.

In this third session when you go out to work on your legs, warm up emphasizing your leg stretches. Especially concentrate on the quadriceps (the quadriceps extensor is the front thigh muscle which joins at the knee on a single tendon and extends the lower leg), a muscle which is not fully utilized in running. We sometimes refer to it affectionately as the puller because it pulls us forward.

Also concentrate on the hamstring stretches. The hamstring, or as it used to be known, "the great tendon," sits on each side of the space in back of the knee and thigh.

Of course your feet will be in on the act—as well as your other parts—but now try to isolate and concentrate on, the legs.

The pictures of Susan Finley will help here. These are stills posed in sequence to give

[1] Gale, Bill, Reports of a Test of Members of the Lake Erie Club in The Wonderful World of Walking, Delta, New York, p. 99.

[2] Franklin, Barry A., Ph.D., Kaimal, Krishna P. Ph.D., Moir, Thomas W., M.D., Hellerstein, Herman K., M.D., Characteristics of National-Class Race Walkers, The Physician and Sportsmedicine, vol. 9, no. 9, September 1981, pp. 101, 106.

[3] Sheehan, George A., M.D., Dr. Sheehan on Running, Bantam New York, p. 33.

left leg is the supporting leg, :ked—body supported over it.

Right knee drives back leg forward. Note how right arm swings back in opposition.

Right leg straightens, knee locks, heel grabs ground.

ght has shifted to the new traight supporting leg. Right niddle of forward swing.

Left knee bends as left leg swings forward.

Arms are almost at maximum swing. Feet are almost at a spread-out heel-toe position.

clear idea of the animated racewalker as seen from the side. In the first, her left leg is the supporting leg; it is straight. The knee is locked and the rest of her body is supported over it.

What happens next (though not shown in a photo), is a slight push off the ball of the trailing (right) foot. In the second photo, the knee has driven the trailing leg forward, reaching out.

In the third picture, the now advancing leg straightens, the knee locks almost stilt-like and she grabs the ground with her right heel. Note how the hip thrusts forward for a longer stride.

The photo on this page shows what happens next:

As she grabs the ground with her right heel, the calves and quadriceps (front thigh muscles) *pull through*, while the now trailing foot begins the push off again. This *pull-through* propels you forward. In this spread-out, heel-toe position the back leg push is almost straight into the ground and back, propelling you again. Don't let it push you upward (bouncing or lifting), only forward.

In the fourth photo, Susan has shifted her weight onto her now straight support leg. And in pictures five and six, the pull-forward, push-back cycle begins anew.

Remember, it is desirable to begin each racewalking cycle with a straight extended leg and the angled foot. If you start straight, you won't have to worry about the pull back; your knee will be ready to lock into place. This keeps you from the Groucho-Glide or the Chuck Berry "Duck" Crouch.

Also remember that when you want to switch your focus from form to speed, the speed will come automatically from the correct form. Speed results from a straight leg and a wide stride, with each leg alternately repeating its pull-push function. This is what's so great about racewalking: there is always an action to move you along. It is virtually pause-free movement at its purest, almost like swimming through air.

Arms—Session IV

Let's stroll down memory lane to your first racewalking session (Chapter 2) when you were a mere novice. That's when you first

Spread-out heel-toe position.

The Groucho Glide.

learned to pump your arms in *The Piston* or *Pusher* method and saw how that action increased your speed. Since we are going to be paying particular attention to the use of the arms, this is a good time to review those early instructions as well as to introduce some new information.

On your first racewalking session, you discovered for yourself:

• How your arms naturally swing in opposition to your legs when you are walking normally. They move you forward and help you with balance.

• That when you increase the swing in your arms, this in turn increases the speed of your legs—the movement in your arms makes your feet move faster.

• This increased swing in the arms is like the action of a pendulum.

• And that as you further increase the speed of this pendulum, the arms start to bend at the elbow, forming an "L" shape which we refer to as *The Piston* or *The Pusher*.

Remember?

You form your hands into loose fists and, concentrating on a point in front of you, swing those fists, punching them upward in rhythm with each step. These are the *basics*.

Remember, whether you racewalk or walk normally, your arms and legs move in relation to one another—*in opposition*. This opposition is important in life, but in racewalking, it's *élan vital*.

We hope you crawled around a lot when you were a baby, because movement studies have shown that a baby's natural progression from lying to walking first must pass through the stage of crawling, because *crawling provides the vital experience of moving in opposition*. So people who have somehow skipped the crawling stage in their early development and gone too quickly from lying in the crib to walking erect have an opposition problem. They tend to move the *same* arm and leg forward when they walk, and they have a stiff unnatural gait. This habit can easily be corrected by putting them through the crawling stage—yes, even as adults.

Instant therapy: Go into a room, close the door, get down on all fours, and crawl around. You don't need diapers and rattles; you don't have to go that far . . . the only regression here is in regard to the act of crawling. The idea is to "crawl-walk" around for a few minutes until you fully experience opposition and what that feels like.

A little while ago, in the session that focused on your torso, we introduced the idea that your arms may be longer than you thought. We suggested that you imagine the movement of your arms initiated not at the shoulder but from your upper spine. Now pay attention to the *scapula*, that bumpy bone or "blade" which protrudes below each shoulder. This is the socket for the arm, even though the movement of the arm actually starts further down your spine: When your arms move, yes, of course your shoulders move, too, but as a result of action in your lower spine.

More about this later, but first here's an easy technique to find the rhythm of the arm movement in relation to your gait and speed:

Start walking. Bend your left arm, and hold your left shoulder with it, hand hooked over the shoulder so your palm rests on the collarbone. Allow your elbow to hang down like a dead weight. Now, do the same with your right arm, and walk around a bit.

If you're not tensing up, you'll feel each shoulder moving in opposition to your forward leg. Your arms *want* to do this. As you continue this exercise, try to locate—sensing from the inside out—where this movement in the shoulders is coming from. You should be able to sense the movement in your spine.

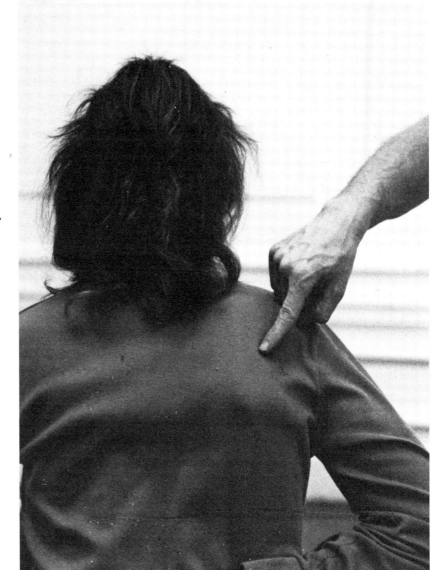

The scapula.

And now, here's a fascinating piece of information: remember that we told you your arms were longer than you thought? Well, they're even longer than we told you they were.

The arm connects to the scapula or shoulder blade as we said, and continues down to the bottom of your spine by means of the latissimus dorsi muscle—and making other connections on down through the pelvis and into the heel of the opposite foot! So when we talk to you about opposition we're not just whistling Dixie. Your opposite foot and arm are *actually connected on a diagonal*. This diagonal moves through bones, muscles and organs.

Perhaps the easiest way to experience this diagonal connection is to stand up, place your feet almost a yard apart, and reach your arms up so that your body forms an "X." Then stretch up a little further to the left and feel the internal dynamic of the force between your left arm and your right foot. Then try reaching your right arm up, noticing the same stretch running through from your right arm to left foot. (Note: "The Diagonal" and the "Five-Pointed Star" warmup exercises in Chapter 13 are also useful for toning and locating the "X" connection of the body muscles.)

In rhythmic motion, this diagonal force of natural opposition can contribute more power, speed, and balance to your racewalking form. Body movement analysts believe that this diagonal is a primary force in the human body since it provides the maximum stimulus of "neurological firing." This means it activates the largest amount of muscle movements.[1]

Not only are the arms the form signature of the racewalker, but, when used properly, they become a secret weapon for speed. In your *piston* motion, which is part of the dynamic diagonal, don't neglect the *backswing* of the elbow in order to favor the forward punch of your hand. Remember that a pendulum swings equally *forward and back*: forward on the upswing, back on the backswing. If you lessen your backswing, your forward punch will be weaker.

And so, without further ado, you are now ready for our secret weapon for gaining speed: If you give a little push back at the furthest extension of the backswing, that little push in the *arm* will help drive the forward *foot* further! We call this the Second Law of Racewalking Thermodynamics: A push backward propels you forward. Isn't that amazing, all you Newtonians?

Enough physics. Let's get outside and do some roadwork on your arms. Let's get those pistons pumping.

Bear in mind:

• The natural feeling of ease in any movement comes from learning the basics and relaxing into the movement.

• If you feel you've lost the sense of arm/leg opposition, start all over again by building from your normal walk.

• Try not to tense your arms . . . it will produce fatigue. Think of the arm swing as beginning in the shoulder blades and spine and allow your arms to relax enough so that they can respond to the impulses from the spine.

• Bend your arms at the elbows: Fully extended arms take longer to move, and take more effort as well. (The swifter and shorter the arms, the faster the legs.)

• The arm level action is low, the shoulders are down and settled. Now is not the time to shrug your shoulders.

• Keep the thrust of the arm swings forward and parallel to that imaginary punching bag in front of you. If the arms angle out too much from your sides or if they cross over the midline of the chest, the motion will force you *sideways* rather than forward. Professor Harold Danish suggests that you demonstrate this to yourself by racewalking with only one arm moving. Wing it. Pump both arms, then just one arm. You'll be pushed inexorably *sideways*. Why? You just removed its *opposition*.

Pump the right arm, and you angle off to your left! Whoops! Pump the left and you go right! It's like a canoe with one paddle. You have to alternate the push or you'll be going in circles. So pump parallel. It'll keep you in balance.

• Relax the torso so that it can swing with the opposition and respond more easily to the impulse and power provided by the *piston*.

• Find a *walk-rhythm* between your feet and your arms. Slow it down. Speed it up. Play with it and improvise.

Pump, pump, pump, pump. . . .

Getting tired? Arms not chugging away at a terrific pace? Relax, here's something to revive you:

Imagine as you're walking that your hands and arms are reaching out in front of you and grabbing a set of parallel ropes. This easier version of the *Piston* helps you to pull yourself along. Really use your hands to grab: grab and pull, grab and pull. . . .

It works! Just go with the image and you'll be zipping on down the road faster than Marcel Marceau.

---

[1] According to Bartenieff Movement, instructor E. G. Shapiro.

Zipping with BIP.

Feet—Session V

There's a characteristic twentieth century adage which goes: *Form follows function*. So now we may ask: What is the function of the feet? Ask any chimpanzee; we haven't progressed that far from our simian relatives. We still grasp the ground with our feet, just as if we were still wearing "hands" on our legs.

Take a look at a cat when it kneads the ground or some other surface such as a sofa (or your lap) with its paws. See how every part of its paw, from the pad to the claws, makes contact with that sofa (or lap). In racewalking, our feet hug the ground in a similar way; we use every part of the foot—heel, ball, and toe. The straight, knee-locked front leg comes down so that the foot is flexed and the heel digs into the ground. At this point, the heel is at an angle of 90 degrees from the leg and 30 to 40 degrees from the ground. Mentally, you should aim for the ideal of a 45-degree angle to the ground. The position of the *heel* pulls you forward. Your stride is now at its widest, with the *ball* of the foot of your trailing leg planted on the ground behind you, *toes* pushing off when the leg is straightened.

This is the *pull/push* we were talking about in the leg session earlier, when the front leg pulls the body up to it, while the advancing leg pushes the body forward. And this is the brief moment when both feet are on the ground.

As the body moves forward, the front foot rolls down, favoring its outside edge all the way from the *heel* to the *ball* of the foot to the *toes*. Please see Richard Goldman's triple exposure photo on page 31.

Rolling down from the outer edge of the heel and foot helps to avoid excessive pronation (flattening of the feet). The outer edge of the foot is its stronger edge, and so is best able to withstand the weight of your step.

Don't forget that at this point your body's weight has shifted to the top of this foot, which is now the base of your supporting leg. The trailing foot is leaving the ground. Remember that the toe of the rear foot doesn't leave the ground until the heel of the advancing foot is firmly planted on the ground in front of it.

When the knee moves the trailing foot through the center, the foot is pointed, though not rigidly. You may want to think of this as a reverse of the front foot flex with the toe pointed downward instead of up.

Finally, when the trailing leg becomes the front leg and straightens, its foot then flexes, the heel digging into the ground to begin the walking cycle all over again.

Here are some helpful hints to remember:

30

The racewalker's legs in motion (note quadriceps muscles). Photo: Richard Goldman

• Grip the ground with your feet so that you feel it moving along beneath you, as if with each step you are pushing the ground behind and away from you. (In this image, *you* are moving the ground.)

• The knee should be over the foot and the feet should be parallel to each other. In other words, don't walk like a duck with toes point-ing outward. True, Charlie Chaplin did well with this walk, he made millions of dollars, and achieved worldwide fame . . . but as far as we know, he never won a walking contest.

• You might find this technique difficult at first, but experienced racewalkers walk a straight line. They do not place each foot *exactly* in front of the other, but they approxi-

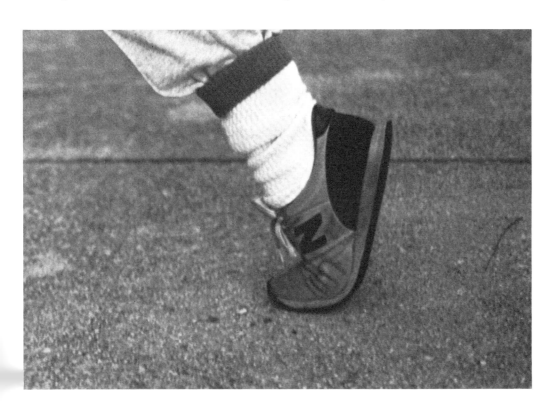

Heel walking—a good exercise for shins and calves.

Walking the line.

mate a straight line as their feet move forward. You can aim for this straightforward direction by imagining that you are walking along a white line three inches wide.

• A good exercise to develop the muscles of the front shins and the calves is to walk on your heels.

This is an excellent conditioner for your 90-degree angle flex. Since the shin muscles are used in this flex—raising and lowering the front of the foot—soreness in the shins is one of the few things walkers occasionally complain about.

• Another simple exercise: walking in place.

This means you perform ordinary walking motions with your feet, but you don't go anywhere because you don't lift your toes off the ground. Just feel the flex.

• Another easy exercise is rotating the foot in a circle, using the ankle as the center of motion.

Walking in place—feel the flex.

Rotate each foot first clockwise, then counter-clockwise. Very relaxing.

When you go out for this session's walk, start by using *just* your feet. The thrill of it all is to forget your hands, and take a tip from Stepinfetchit: "Feet, do your stuff!" Start normally, then angle your front foot, grip the ground, and pull through. Roll off from the front to the back, the toe to the heel, using the outside of the foot. Your speed should increase. This is the primal experience of walking: feeling the ground with your paw.

You can use this technique in daily life as an undercover racewalking exercise. It's really fun, and truly astonishing in its effect. You have to experience it yourself to believe it. It looks like you're just walking, strolling along—but you're outdistancing everybody in sight, virtually gliding along like a sailboat launched by the strongest wind.

The Head— Session VI

Think of someone who moves perfectly, like Fred Astaire. Look at some of his old movies. He seems so relaxed: his legs, his arms, his shoulders, his head. He jumps, leaps, and seems to soar through space effortlessly. Sometimes his feet are going a mile a minute. It's got to be hard, yet it looks so easy. What does he have? Aside from talent and years of technique, he's got *style*. He's found his own way of being light as the proverbial feather, despite his earthly weight, despite gravity, despite anything.

How can we feel even a little bit like Fred Astaire when we racewalk? We can *think* light, for starters.

Think "light as air"; it will help shape your movement because thoughts influence motivations and desires. So think thoughts that will help keep your head held high. And the way to think is *up*. Think Peter Pan. Pretend there's a wire on you, and the stage hands are hoisting you up—not enough to lift your feet off the ground, just high enough to straighten you out nicely, giving your spine a good stretch. So straight up you go, with your feet still on the ground. Now *that's* "thinking tall."

You've heard the Shakespearean quotation, "Uneasy lies the head that wears a crown. . ." Why is the head uneasy? One reason could be because it's *heavy*: not just the crown, but the head itself. That's why lots of people's heads hang down. We haven't weighed ours lately, but someone whispered "20 pounds." And that sounds about right to us.

In fact, keeping the head up high and balanced is one of nature's wonders. It's a balancing act, like keeping plates twirling on a stick. True, there are muscles to support it, but essentially the head is *balanced* on top of the spine. Relax your neck muscles and over falls the head. (You can check this out by doing the head roll exercise.)

In the torso session, we offered you the balloon image, thinking of your head as a helium balloon floating upward to help you align your spine straight toward the ceiling. Now try it again, this time concentrating on the *distance* you feel between your tail bone (at the bottom of the spine) and the top of your head. Your entire spine should now feel longer. Try this as you racewalk.

Another way to achieve this elongated feeling is to imagine a pole moving up through the vertebrae, lengthening each "building block" connection. When the pole reaches your neck, slow it down and feel the pole beginning to balance your head on your top vertebra. We find that if you look for this balance—making very tiny adjustments in your neck and head (close your eyes, rotating your head ever so slightly until it arrives at its most perfect position)—your head will tell you when it reaches the very pinnacle of your spine. It will say, "That feels good. I want to sit *there*."

In racewalking, if the head is bent forward or back, it causes unnecessary tension. It can drag your shoulders down or tilt you back. And if you lead with your jaw . . . more tension.

So remember the balloon, remember the stagehands, Peter Pan, and the wire, remember the pole, but most of all remember Fred Astaire and balance that head.

Putting It All Together—Session VII

Thus far we have concentrated on helping you discover what the best form is and how to achieve it. And when you put it all together your way, it becomes *your* style. Each walker has a different style—a distinctive way of moving within the rules. It is only when you compete with other walkers that judgments enter the picture. Remember, the rules say that you must maintain contact with the ground, that the advanced foot must make contact before the rear foot breaks contact, and that the leg must be straight.

The two rule-breakers to watch out for are called *lifting* and *creeping*. Lifting happens when both feet are off the ground and judges feel the contestant is running. This often occurs at the finish of a race, usually caused by a too rigid torso or incorrect foot placement. When your leg is at its greatest extension is the time to watch out for this. Racers have been known to fly above the ground like hovercraft. Results? Disqualification and international incidents.

Creeping happens when the knees are bent as in a normal walk instead of being straight or locked. A walker should make an effort to straighten the forward leg as soon as it ad-

vances through the center point. Creeping often occurs without one's being aware of it, usually because of fatigue. If you were in a race, warnings and disqualification would result.

We're not recommending that you go out and race right away, but we do recommend that you establish your good habits now so that if and when you do decide to compete, your form won't get in your way. Even if you don't choose to compete, you can't go far fast without good form.

Our purpose here was to give you lots of material to play with—exercises, theories, suggestions—that might help you as you work with each part of your body. Take what you need from this chapter and test it out. If it works for you, use it. If it doesn't, forget it or come back to it later. Maybe something we mentioned seemed too complex, or even too simple. It's all right. Don't let anything throw you. We don't want to transform you into a version of the centipede who became hopelessly confused when asked how he walked. Just remember you've always walked, you've already racewalked, and all we wish you to do now is enjoy it as much as we do.

In this last session we shall offer you a list of reminders—key elements of movement to concentrate on while racewalking. The coordination between the key elements will happen automatically as you shift your awareness from one to the other. Concentrate on each one then move on to the next. If you find yourself at a plateau, don't worry about it. Little by little you will come to experience the logic of each of the physical sensations described in this chapter.

One reason we are so fascinated with the sport is that it seems so easy, and yet involves so many levels of awareness. Eventually, all the elements—thoughts and actions—will combine into an efficient, rhythmic, and individual style that is all yours.

ink light as air.

Key Elements

1. Lead and land your forward moving leg on the heel.
2. Point foot straight ahead, toes pointing up, flexed.
3. Keep front leg straight (locked knee) as you pull it back.
4. Follow up with the foot rolling through (the pull/push begins).
5. Maintain opposition of arms and legs, each countering the other.
6. Bend arms at 90 degrees. The piston action pushes you along.
7. The faster you move your arms, the faster your legs will go. Don't tense the shoulders or rib cage.
8. Bend knee only as your leg moves forward.
9. Bend only one knee at a time (the other leg is always straight).
10. Lengthen your stride with a forward thrust of your hip. Longer stride equals greater speed.
11. Lift from the pelvis, sit on the hips for correct posture and a smooth gliding gait.
12. Don't arch your back, extend your tail, or break forward at the waist.
13. Keep your head upright (not stiff) and balanced on your spine like a floating balloon.
14. Think *tall*. Think *up*.
15. Place your steps one in front of another—walking the line.
16. Keep feet parallel. Don't splay or duck-walk.
17. Let your feet skim close to the ground. Hug the road.
18. Remember, think flexible: "forward, up, and over" with your hips.
19. Keep the pelvic motion fluid. Rotation is from front to back, not side to side. Don't wiggle. Proper technique leads to faster speeds and smoother walking.
20. Let the energy-flow in one part of the body be transformed into power for the whole body.
21. Don't tense, push, or force it, even during a race. Relax into the effort.

Don't give up. Don't get lazy. Don't get sloppy. With patience and practice you will master the technique. After all, as we said before: The racewalking form is the most efficient and effective way of walking fast based on your body's natural movements.

CHAPTER 5

THE RACEWALKER IN TRAINING

"Several major medical studies have shown that aerobic exercise like racewalking leads to a longer, healthier life. People who engage in such activities have less heart disease and live longer."

—LAWRENCE J. COHN, M.D.
CARDIOLOGIST

When athletes hear the word "training," it's music to their ears. You say "train" to an athlete, the athlete answers "where?" and is off and running—or racewalking—in search of the latest most rigorous muscle-taxing regimen to be devised.

When non-athletes hear the word "training," they become oddly uneasy. When you say "train" to a non-athlete, the non-athlete answers "why?" and is off and running—or taking a cab—in the opposite direction. This is how we felt as neophyte racewalkers.

You athletes might want to skip ahead a few pages and start training. All others: We'd like to share with you some insights about the meaning of the word "train." Our dictionary[1] provides four meanings, which suggested to us four different approaches—which helped us overcome our fear of training. Herewith, we offer them to you:

1. "to cause to grow as desired": For example, muscle development can grow from soft and flabby to lean and hard.

2. "to form by instruction, discipline, or drill": We must confess this one used to upset us, conjuring up visions of algebra tables, basic training in the Marines, and learning anything by rote. Then we realized this needn't mean torture at all, but simply the use of repetition which is the core of all learning, such as going out almost every day to racewalk in the open air.

3. "to make or become prepared (as by exercise) for a test of skill": This means of course preparing for a race or other event. It doesn't have to be a long race or a marathon; it can be a short local race amongst friends or it could even be a *self-imposed* test of skill, such as, "By next month I'm going to go ten miles."

4. "to aim or point at an object": To us this means selecting one's training objective(s). This can take many forms.

Keeping in mind the four different approaches, let us concentrate on the fourth one and see how it encompasses the other three. Selecting training objectives might be a vague process at first, but it can become a process of growth and change. In other words, at first you might not be too sure what your objectives *are*, which is fine; they will reveal themselves to you. After you think you have your objective(s)

The *Merriam Webster Dictionary*, Simon and Schuster Pocket Books, New York, 1974.

37

clearly in mind, you might find that they have changed. Perhaps sharing our objectives with you will help you clarify this process for yourself.

Our Objectives

William started out with a vague feeling that racewalking would help him to release work-related tension. His first goal for this purpose was a modest one mile a day. After several weeks the racewalking experience revealed to him that in addition to tension release, this was an ideal way to experience heightened body consciousness and draw upon hidden reserves of energy. Then these became his objectives, and he realized that four miles every other day at a faster pace seemed to be the way to accomplish this.

Marion started out with a specific objective, to lose weight (in conjunction with a diet), because she had learned that the best diet programs involved exercise. After going one mile a day, six days a week, for a month, she had lost five pounds and was encouraged to try two miles. At first she didn't know exactly why she wanted to go two miles, which had once seemed an impossibility, but once she found she could do this with ease, she realized the true reason was a sense of accomplishment in a field she had never considered before. In the process of moving up to six miles a day, she discovered new muscle tone, weight loss, and a new body image.

Your Objectives

Some objectives include: distance, endurance, speed, competition, fitness (including psychological fitness such as release of tension and positive self-image), improved appearance, and recovery from injury. Many of these ob-jectives are true for other sports as well, but of all popular sports, recovery from injury is unique to swimming and racewalking. In fact, for healing athletes, racewalking—because of its accessibility—is the sport of choice. For such an athlete, the objective is to keep going while on the mend.

Whatever you think your objectives are at first, they will be revealed as you go along. Even if you are not sure about what you want to accomplish, you will discover this by going out and doing it.

How far can you expect to go at first?

A mile is a respectable distance for new, non-athletic racewalkers. If you measure off a mile on your territory, and even that seems too great a distance at first, try half a mile.

When we started out four summers ago, a mile racewalk on the boardwalk seemed a great accomplishment. Even warming up deserved a gold medal. We picked a bright blue and yellow wooden building as our turn-around, half-mile marker. To get to it was our first training goal. It would take us 15 minutes to get there and ten to get back. For some reason the trip back was always faster, perhaps because we chatted, gossiped, and laughed on the way out. Then gradually the process of the exercise took over, so that by the time we turned back we had moved beyond talk and the rhythm of our pace had quieted us down. Sometimes, when we had missed a few sessions or on a blah day we felt so out of shape that even at our slow speed we'd have to stop and pause and stroll for a while. Now, thanks to our training, we racewalk the whole boardwalk, a mile each way, as many times as we want at 12 or 1 minutes a mile, passing our blue and yellow building with ease.

How fast should you go at first?

As new walkers, you might start out with half-hour sessions for the first weeks of your training. Your goal might be to walk a mile in 20 minutes. If it takes longer, it takes longer. Don't worry about it. Wear your watch and time yourself for the mile, then try to shave off a minute each time you go out. But don't go so fast that you lose your form.

Do the mile, but *do the mile in style!*

Remember, at the beginning form is all, form is content, form is the ticket.

The two-miler and how to pace it:

It will vary from walker to walker but generally, after about a month (or less) if you've been going out at least three times a week, you will be ready and even eager to do a two-miler. Two miles in the total picture of a long distance sport doesn't seem like much (the 50K Olympic Racewalk is 31 miles!) but to us when we began, it seemed like a vast wooden pathway stretching ever outwards. To us, two miles meant going past the blue and yellow house and vanishing into a point on the horizon we couldn't even see.

Athletes who have skipped the first few pages of this chapter can tune back in now.

Doing two miles is the beginning of real training. Why? Because it involves a new strategy: pacing for distance. Seasoned athletes know that the usual beginner's error is to go out fast and hard (as in a race). This enthusiasm is welcome on the way out, but unwise. A better strategy would be to save some of that energy for the way home. Pacing is the key: parcelling out your energy. Even a slow start may pay off, allowing you to plug into hidden reserves on the way back.

One way to tell if your pacing is too fast is the "rule of mouth": you should be able to talk and converse in complete sentences with your companion or, if alone, to yourself. And the conversation shouldn't be too choppy or short-winded, either. This might be one reason racewalkers seem more gregarious than runners: They talk more. They have to, because

they're testing their pace, as well as enjoying each other's company. Another way of measuring pacing, "Am I going fast or slow?" is the *pulse* test. This is also a useful technique to check on your aerobic fitness level, although lately some doctors disagree.

The Pulse Test

Get ready for some advanced math. Subtract your age from the number 220. The result should give you the maximum heart rate attainable for your age range. The theory is that you lose a beat from this maximum heart rate every year. The theoretical objective with aerobic exercise is to reach a pulse rate between 70 percent and 80 percent of your maximum heart rate. Please note: This is not a hard and fast rule; there can be considerable heart rate differences in "fit" individuals of the same age. However, it is usually a helpful indication, and we find it fun to do.

A resting pulse rate is obtained by taking your pulse during a period of relaxation and inactivity, such as watching TV (reruns are good), sitting in the bath, or just lying in bed under boring circumstances. Some say to do this just upon awakening. To take your pulse, use a watch with a second hand, press your fingers (not your thumb, which has its own detectable pulse) on your wrist just below the thumb, or on the large veins on each side of the neck. Count the beats for ten seconds and multiply by six to determine your pulse for a minute.

On your next workout, take your pulse for ten seconds, either during the workout or *right after* you stop. Don't wait, because the pulse tends to fall rapidly, to seek its resting state as soon as bodily exertion stops. Multiply the number of beats by six, and you've arrived at your *active pulse rate.* Remember, the active pulse rate should be between 70 and 80 percent of your maximum heart rate.

For example, a 33-year-old person has a theoretical maximum heart rate of 187. Seventy percent of that is approximately 130 beats per minute. So if that person is not getting 130 beats per minute racewalking, then he/she is not receiving aerobic benefits. There may be other physical benefits, psychological benefits, and even some weight loss, but according to this theory, such a person is not really doing an aerobic activity.

Nick Bdera, U.S. 50K racewalking Masters' champ and Olympic hopeful, takes a high-tech approach to monitoring his pulse. He works out with a portable heart rate monitor strapped to his chest, which gives him a constant reading of his heart rate. He wears this while training to keep himself racewalking at a maximal rate.

Taking the pulse rate during or right at the end of a workout provides an interesting reward for your effort. Although its scientific validity is not up to us to determine, we derive a strange but undeniable source of pleasure from coming in after a workout and fingering our arteries with a clear sense of purpose.

Approaching the Longer Distances: Three Training Methods

Since racewalking is considered a distance sport, depending on your objectives you may now wish to extend your mileage. You may have arrived at such an objective through your two-mile experience, or you may have carried your long distance goals over from a previous sport such as running. You may desire to build stamina and cover additional ground with a more strenuous workout. Or you may just want to increase your speed.

In any case, here are three training methods which can be used for a variety of purposes.

1. *Intervals:* The principle of interval training is to increase the amount of time in which you are going at a fast pace while gradually reducing the amount of time spent at a slow or resting pace. Interval training is useful for long distance or endurance workouts. In order to work out with interval training, you need to either mark off a series of equal distances along your route or use a watch.

Some examples of equal distances are: quarter-mile landmarks, half-mile landmarks, four city blocks, one-mile landmarks, or 220 and 440 yards on a track. Determine your distance objectives, such as quarter-mile intervals for three miles, half-mile intervals for four miles, six 220 laps, or choose your own. For example, if you picked a quarter-mile segment for your first interval, you should build up slowly until your muscles are in the groove, then increase your speed until you are racewalking at a satisfyingly brisk pace. When you pass your first interval marker, slow down to a resting pace to recover from your brisk speed.

And as you approach your next interval mark, increase your pace until you're back to your fast speed again. Repeat this *fast . . . slow . . . fast* until you complete your distance objective.

If you don't have a series of marked equal distances, you can use a segment of time instead. Time becomes your interval measure. For example: . . . *four minutes fast . . . three minutes slow.* Some athletes try to approach their active pulse rates during the fast interval in order to monitor their efforts: *three minutes fast . . . two minutes slow.* Try to reduce the amount of time devoted to resting and recovery; increase the time for speed and endurance.

Decrease the slow, increase the fast. But unless you're already accustomed to stresses of marathons or marathon-like endeavors, we don't recommend pushing yourself to exhaustion or into breathlessness. Avoid resting too much (while racewalking). Don't just stroll and then go like crazy. Such extremes can actually harm you.

2. *Repetitions:* Repetitions are a variation of interval training. This method is often used for those working on speed. The fastest mile for a racewalk is somewhere around five minutes, 40 seconds. The 1983 New York Marathon winning time for racewalking was three hours and 19 minutes—that's for a little over 26 miles. These are times set by world class walkers, but they'll give you an idea of what to aim for while working on your speed repetitions.

In repetition training, the basic idea is an increase of speed for every other interval. As before, mark off your equal intervals either by time segments, landmarks, or yards, then racewalk the first interval at a warmup (slower than normal) speed. When you reach the second interval, shift to a speed that is lower than your best possible speed. Take the third interval at a resting pace (but not too slow), and as you approach the fourth interval, pick up your pace. Do the fourth *faster* than you did the second. If you feel you can go even faster, slow down, and then take your next interval at your *fastest* possible speed. Finally, warm down with an easy breathing stride.

The repetitive technique—slow start, swift speed, slow recovery, swifter speed—is employed to gradually accustom the well-trained walker to the competitive faster pacing of races. The theory is that by gradually accelerating for longer periods of time (shortening the rest periods) the body's tolerance to heart/lung exertion (or stress) increases. The resting periods are designed to lessen fatigue, especially at the beginning of training.

Fartlek

This delightful word, one of our favorites in any language, represents a delightful practice. It means "speed-play" in Swedish, and was originated by Gösta Holmer to free runners from tedious training regimes, but has since been adapted by racewalkers. We have encountered two varieties of fartleks: One is an equivalent of a runner's sprint training: you do a short burst of very fast racewalking between two close (such as ten to 20 yards) points. The other kind of fartlek is used for longer (up to several miles) distances, in which you follow your instincts and do varieties of speed rhythms—much like playing jazz riffs on a musical theme. For example: fast, slo-o-ow, fast-fast, slow down, charge up a hill, stretch your arms while you walk, circle back, scale that hill again, long-stride down it, shift gears, and slow down.

Both kinds of fartleks are used for preparation for fast one- to two-mile races, as well as for fast finishes in longer competitions. Fartleks also provide an ideal mental setting for conquering the often agonizing process of dealing with hills.

There is an indefinable something about a fartlek. After all the attention to proper form, after all the mileage, after all the steady pacing and timing and training, you can just let go— and as William experienced firsthand, it's the closest you can get to *flying*. Not bad for a sport where your feet are on the ground.

Racewalking With Weights

Many racewalkers get to the point where they wish to increase strength and endurance, and a logical step seems to be the use of weights as they racewalk. William wanted to work specifically on the endurance capacity of his arm muscles. Since repeated muscular contractions are involved in racewalking, and since endurance stems from building muscle strength (or the ability of the muscles to contract), he used lightweight dumbbells during his workouts. Heavy weights add bulk; light ones are the best for increased muscle tone and contraction conditioning.

The weights were the add-on variety—a pound each—which enabled the load to be increased from two to six pounds for each hand. This fits right in with accepted weight-training technique: when the load feels too easy, add weight.

In traditional racewalking form, hold one weight in each hand, and continue to pump in piston motion with your arms for about 15 to 30 minutes or one to two miles. This was an immense help in developing William's arm swing; the weights have loosened his swing and given the arms a tight, punching dynamic.

Another way of working with weights is a fartlek-like maneuver, with variations that have little in common with the traditional racewalking arm positions: You can pump your arms directly in front of you, or pump them above your head while holding the weights for short periods of time (say, two minutes). This releases any tension which might be caused by the usual repetitive pumping motion, and provides a different type of resistance and stretch.

You can choose to wear strap-on ankle weights to increase muscle strength in your legs. One to two pounds is generally sufficient. This can cause painfully pulled muscles, however—which happened to a friend of ours—so we advise caution with leg weights.

But the secret thrill of carrying weights for your arms is first you use them, then you don't.

Alternate arms and legs.

Raise arms straight up.

First you use them. . . .

The direct contrast between an intense workout with weights until you're so used to them you feel they're almost a part of you—with the freedom you experience when you put them down and continue to work out without them—is astonishing. Your arms feel almost weightless, like they're floating. The pumping action is easier and faster than ever before. You're soaring! You've become the jet-propelled racewalker.

Going the Distance: The Long Walks

The racewalking question, to go or not to go long distance, inevitably arises. Sooner or later two miles, even four miles, is nothing to the well-conditioned racewalker. Ex-long distance runners in particular might find themselves at this stage. The question then becomes, "How do I train for longer distances?"

The best training method we have found for longer distances is to build up to your specific long distance goal by halves. For example, if you wish to racewalk a 20 kilometer (12.4 mile) distance, your first training objective would be to build up to six-mile workouts as your base training distance (B.T.D.).

This level should be maintained for at least a week before increasing any further distance. Two weeks would be even better. If the six-mile level is difficult at first, try alternating training periods of six- and four-mile limits. Please remember that dedicated athletes in training go out *consistently* every day. So if you wish to achieve longer distances, four times a week is the minimum. If you happen to miss a week, don't be discouraged, just build up gradually again as soon as possible.

Note: One helpful device you might want to use to keep track of your progress is a personal training diary, especially if you wish to work on your time. For competition training, this is probably a necessity. We suggest you buy an inexpensive (or exorbitant, if you prefer) day-by-day pocket size diary. Then for each day's entry, include the following:

- your distance
- the time it took you to traverse it
- your pulse rate (optional)
- if it was a good day and why
- if it was a bad day and why

In analyzing good or bad days, don't be judgmental, but try to be as subjective as possible. Use your instincts. Did you take any extra vitamins? Did you eat differently? Did you sleep more or less or in a different bed? Don't forget the more objective answers, too, such as weather conditions, the route you took, etc.

When you are able to do six miles comfortably, you should immediately set your sights on nine miles. By rule-of-halves, this will be your new distance plateau. A simple way to accomplish this is to add an additional mile to your six-mile B.T.D. at least one day a week. If you reach ten miles, and can repeat it again within the next few days, you will find your 12-mile objective within reach.

Racewalker Susan Friess Goldman provides an excellent example of this training practice. She was used to a six-mile standard. She increased the number of *times* she went out a week, and thus extended her mileage. What was her objective? At that time she was determined to enter a half-marathon of 13.1 miles, and although racing was not her primary racewalking goal, she felt this was a good challenge and a way to improve her overall training output.

As she says, "I kept going five or six miles each day. I wasn't setting a goal of miles at first, I was setting a goal of increased number of days . . . after a few weeks I started adding to the number of miles one day a week. Most every day, I was doing five or six miles. On Sunday, I went to seven miles instead of six, and the following week I went to eight miles."

Keep in mind that when Susan started training almost four years ago she racewalked a mile in 20 minutes (just like we did when we started). Her training over the years has brought her mile speed down to 12 minutes, and enabled her to accomplish a half-marathon in two hours and 42 minutes—a goal within reach of most racewalkers who follow this training schedule.

Of course this schedule can be extended to full marathon training, or any mileage goal you pursue. Just keep adding those miles one by one, week by week. At the beginning, training may seem hard to do, but once you start it will become part of your daily life, and you will find that when you don't do it, you actually miss it.

"Racewalking looks brutal, but you're not pounding the ground and lifting your body in the air as a runner does with each step. You race down on the ground, and it doesn't tire you out as quickly. When you get going at high speed and your arms are whipping, it's kind of an illusion that people look at and say, 'Wow, look at those knees and hips and those arms going like crazy.' But it's not that bad, really!"

—RON LAIRD, WORLD RECORDHOLDER FOR NATIONAL RACEWALKING CHAMPIONSHIPS, AND COACH FOR THE 1984 U.S. OLYMPIC RACEWALKING TEAM

CHAPTER 6

THE WELL-NOURISHED RACEWALKER

Nutrition Is Crucial

If you come to racewalking from another sport, you probably already have a working knowledge of how a proper diet determines performance. If the idea of *any* activity is new to you, you may not have thought much about diet's *direct relation* to athletic prowess. Perhaps you want to lose weight—or even gain weight.

When we came to racewalking, Marion wanted to lose weight, while William wanted to gain weight. We both wanted to develop muscle; we wanted to be stronger without looking "muscle-bound." And certainly we wanted to be healthier.

Bearing all this in mind, we embarked on research in nutrition. We learned that widespread food processing has silently taken most of the nourishment out of many prepared foods. So if you eat mostly unprocessed, whole foods, you will be in much better shape, avoid any food allergies, and require fewer vitamin mineral supplements—because you will actually be getting some old-fashioned nourishment from everything you eat. This means: whole-grain breads and pastas instead of white bread and pasta, natural cereals and grains instead of prepared, standard "dry" cereals, and fresh vegetables and fruits instead of canned.

We also take vitamin and mineral supplements with our meals. To determine if you need any, which ones, and how much, we recommend study, research, and careful label-reading. Better yet, consult an expert.

The Protein vs. Complex Carbohydrate Controversy

Up until about a decade ago high protein diets were "in," both as a preferred way to lose weight and as a widespread reaction to the growing awareness of hypoglycemia and the dangers of excessive intake of refined sugar. Frequent high protein meals and snacks were likewise "in." Fats and oils were considered OK, too.

Protein was once considered strength-building for sports: remember Rocky drinking all those raw eggs before he went out jogging? (We are referring to Sylvester Stallone's first *Rocky*.) Today we know that raw egg white depletes the body's stores and prevents the absorption of biotin, an essential B vitamin. So don't emulate Rocky before you go out racewalking. In fact, he couldn't help surrounding himself with animal protein—he even punched sides of beef instead of a punching bag.

Now the pendulum has swung to *complex*

carbohydrates as opposed to *simple* carbohydrates, such as refined sugars, also known as *empty calories* and generally Not Good. A large part of this nutritional turnaround has been due to the revolutionary work of Nathan Pritikin and other proponents of low fat diets to help combat heart disease and high blood pressure. This type of diet is now widely recommended for weight loss, general good health, and increased athletic performance.

Complex carbohydrates include vegetables, fruits, and grain products (*whole* grains) such as cereals and pastas. According to Pritikin aficionados, fats and oils are now out, and some say even protein intake should be kept low. If Sylvester Stallone keeps up with this trend, he could be punching fetuccini in *Rocky VIII*.

Protein is needed by the body to repair, build, and promote growth. Recent findings have shown that balanced high protein diets (not extreme, of course) improve mental health. And why not? The brain is an organ and it, too, needs protein to keep it functioning well. Protein is also an excellent purveyor of energy; it keeps you going. You get less hungry after eating proteins than just about any other type of food, hence its reputation for being "filling." This includes vegetable as well as animal and fish proteins unless you're a vegetarian, in which case you should really learn the facts about vegetable proteins.

But too much protein and too little carbohydrate can create a state of chemical imbalance called ketosis, which causes—among other undesirable side effects—a lack of energy. This, of course, is the last thing a racewalker wants.

When all-protein diets were fashionable, some diet/medical circles maintained that a "mild" state of ketosis was not dangerous. They could not have been thinking in terms of athletic performance. People who lost weight on high protein diets found they had to sit around the house a lot. They lost weight, but some of that weight loss included muscle. We now know that complex carbohydrates *build* muscle, which protein alone does not. (In case you're worried about adding weight, racewalking burns 80 to 100 calories per mile.)

Complex carbohydrates supply bulk and fiber, which is currently fashionable for what is tactfully called "elimination." Now the general public has discovered what health food lovers knew all along: Foods as nature originally grew them are necessary for a healthy digestion.

As far as the racewalker is concerned, there is yet another reason to include complex carbohydrates and bulk fiber in the diet. Of all foods, carbohydrates are digested and converted into energy the most quickly.

Complex-carbohydrate lovers say that fats and oils are dangerous, but the cholesterol studies regarding heart disease are constantly being rethought and revised. For healthy athletes, fatty foods are somewhat inefficient since fat takes longer to digest than carbohydrates. But fats and oils also provide Vitamins A and D, especially vital in climates with long cold winters during the months when people get little sunlight. Although fats and oils are not used quickly, they are a vital *stored* form of energy, and this storage facility is useful for the athlete.

We say: Eat whenever you are hungry, never eat gigantic amounts at one time, and be sure to drink enough liquids, never underestimating the value of water.

Après Racewalking

When you are active, you burn a lot more carbohydrates than anything else, so it is appropriate to replace them after a workout. Also you should drink lots of liquids after a workout. We prefer water and natural juices. We are talking about ordinary workouts here, up to ten or 12 miles. Marathoners' needs are more complex.

Under ordinary conditions, stoke that furnace with complex carbohydrates: whole grain cereals, whole grain crackers, fruit, and veggies. And, we say, add some protein to that.

If it's hot and you have sweated a lot, whatever you do, stay away from salt tablets because they can set off a dangerous process of cellular imbalance. When an athlete sweats, the body loses water, salt, Vitamin C, minerals, and electrolytes. All of these must be replaced. For non-marathoners, tomato juice supplies potassium, some Vitamin C, electrolytes, and water. Then a snack and (eventually) a multivitamin and mineral supplement will do on a daily basis.

For the serious and long distance racewalker, a so-called *activity drink* might be a boon. Check the ingredients. The best of these drinks should include glucose, magnesium, calcium, Vitamin C, potassium, and sodium—and always more potassium than sodium. We like a Vitamin C powder which contains the above ingredients. It is available in individual packets which you dissolve in water or juice.

An activity drink with these properties is designed to quench thirst, replace everything the body lost in the workout—and not leave you feeling bloated. After a vigorous workout other liquids, even water, may bloat the stomach and possibly cause cramps. We are talking here of *vigorous* workouts, marathon style—not a daily five-mile racewalk, or less (our category).

Sweets for the Racewalker

"Sugar is a good source of energy." This common belief is still widely held, but it is not accurate really, because *all* food gives you energy. A calorie is in fact a unit of energy, so every time you consume a calorie you are getting energy. But different foods take different amounts of time to provide the *feeling* of energy, and sugar supposedly works the fastest and gets burned up the fastest.

White sugar is the number one villain: tooth destroyer, cavity causer, hyperactivity-hyper, diabetes aggravator, hypoglycemia horrifier, and so forth, ad infinitum. White sugar is found in almost all commercial baked goods, candies, and cereals, and lurks in many other processed foods. Several books have been written on this subject, comparing white sugar to heroin, cocaine, and Satan. We would not go quite that far, but we do advise you to go easy on white or refined sugar. Avoid it when you can, and if you want something sweet, eat a natural substance like fruit, raisins, honey, or fructose, a natural sugar. We are cautious about most artificial sweeteners and soft drinks containing them. We enjoy fruit juices, the new soft drinks made with honey or fructose, and plain water at the end of a long workout.

Before Racewalking

Never eat much just before going out to racewalk. In the morning or when you are *really* hungry, yogurt is excellent—also toast, cereal, raisins, and fruit.

The latest energy fad among runners is caffeine just before a workout. Some athletes act as if they've just discovered coffee, and laud its beneficial effects when drunk just before a race. We are not anti-coffee militants, but we wish to point out that coffee can cause indigestion and it depletes the body of Vitamin C. Today you can find numerous warnings about the hazards of coffee: claims that it can cause heart attacks, ulcers, anxiety neurosis, and many other ills. Everyone's tolerance to coffee is different, but we suggest you go easy with this brew. We used to live on it, we confess, but we've cut down radically, although we still occasionally enjoy a cup. However, we *never* depend on it for racewalking stamina.

Alcohol

Alcohol is not recommended, especially before racewalking, but beer or wine in moderation at other times is your own business. Alcohol is high in calories and also depletes the body of B vitamins and other nutrients, so there are lots of nutritional reasons to be cautious with the intake of this much-discussed liquid.

Glycogen and Carbohydrate Loading

Glycogen is muscle starch, a storage form of glucose. Increased regular use of muscles increases their ability to store glycogen. When marathoners "hit the wall" (which usually happens after about twenty miles), this is believed to be a total glycogen depletion. Extending the glycogen usage is a study in itself, involving complex muscle analyses and pacing for athletes. Essentially, the belief so far is: Sprinters run anaerobically and burn glycogen; "slower" athletes exercise aerobically and burn fat. Racewalking is aerobic and steady-paced, so for all practical purposes it now seems racewalkers hold on to their glycogen stores.

Some may inevitably try the marathoners' ritual of *carbohydrate loading*. While we do not recommend it here, we will explain it. Remember, it is solely a pre-marathon ploy aimed at beating the Wall.

The first four days are devoted to depleting the glycogen stores. The marathoner eats all protein and leaves out the carbos: bread and fruits, most vegetables, as well as sweets, pasta, and other goodies. During the last three days the marathoner eats mostly carbohydrates, culminating in the famous pre-marathon pasta dinner.

Pacing of pre-race mileage must be carefully monitored when carbohydate-loading. There is danger of ketosis during the all-protein period, and the carbo-loading period can aggravate hypoglycemia; it can be hard on the body, and may cause extreme fatigue to some. Books abound on this trendy pre-marathon practice, so study it if you must in more detail—elsewhere. For our part, we say: Eat sensibly at *all* times—yes, especially pre-marathon.

CHAPTER 7

THE WELL-DRESSED RACEWALKER: CLOTHING AND RELATED GEAR

The key word in proper racewalking apparel is "comfort." If you come to racewalking from running, you probably know what to wear on the hoof. Our clothing is not that different. Fortunately the sports fashion industry is booming, thanks to the running craze, so we racewalkers can take advantage of the easy availability of spiffy yet functional racewalking attire. But you don't have to spend a penny for starters. In fact, there are those who say one never should get expensive clothing when you do a sport just for pleasure. (If you're on a team, of course, you have to wear your colors.)

The Basics

SHOES

We will start you from the bottom up, which means shoes first. If this is your first racewalking session, you may wear your sneakers or your most comfortable pair of walking shoes, but preferably you should own a pair of running shoes. At the time of this writing, shoes made specifically for racewalking are not yet on the market, but running shoes are worn with good effect by racewalkers. We will give you a technical chat about selecting a pair of running shoes at the end of this chapter. Good shoes are vital, but we have been known to racewalk barefoot. If you happen to be standing on a beach barefoot as you read this, don't worry about shoes yet.

SOCKS

If you are wearing shoes, you'll need socks. Socks absorb perspiration, prevent blisters, and preserve the life of your shoes. We have heard of a tribe of runners in New York's Central Park who defiantly run sockless, but we suspect that these are probably the same athletes who would lash rubber tires to their feet and run in shorts and tee shirts during a blizzard.

Appropriate socks are thick cotton. The most economical are called tube socks and that's just what they look like—tubes. The best are socks made specifically for sports, often of terrycloth blend with a soft cushion under the foot—and there are many varieties in between. The important thing to remember is to stay away from

The well-dressed racewalker.

nylon or any slippery, non-absorbent substances. Moisture encourages blisters. Let your feet breathe!

There are funny little socks favored by women tennis players in the summer. They nestle within your shoe and are invisible except for a tiny colored pompom which pokes up behind the ankle, supposedly to keep them from slipping. Marion, who has tried them, advises that for longer distances they can slip down into your shoe and you might find yourself racewalking with a painful pompom under your heel.

SHORTS

In moderate climates or indoor tracks you will probably be most comfortable in loose fitting shorts. Any soft cotton shorts are best. They should not be tight or binding anyplace, because this can cause blisters as you move. No belts, of course. Nylon shorts are OK *with cotton* undies. The special shorts made for running and tennis can be wonderful for racewalking, because they usually have slits on the sides which allow for your longer stride and prevent cutting in the crotch.

SWEATPANTS

Sweatpants are usually worn in cooler weather, but sweatpant aficionados wear them in any weather at all. Sweatshirt material is a miracle; in fact, we think it's one of the secret motivations for the athletics boom. People will do anything, it seems, as an excuse to wear this comforting and cuddly fabric which feels a lot like a baby's bunting. Remember Dr. Dentons? Sweatpants are also cheap, and now they come in many lively colors besides the old drab, but serviceable, gray or navy blue. They are large and roomy enough to accommodate the movement of your legs, and they never bind you with a zippered fly or a tight crotch. They're easy to wash; just throw them in the machine and dryer.

RUNNING SUITS

Also known as warmup suits, running suits are a whole new world of attire. You can find them in a variety of weights for various kinds of weather, colors, designs, name designers and prices—which can be quite steep. Their chief benefit, as far as we see it, is psychological— which is nothing to sneeze at. If you feel good, look good, and convey an air of confidence, this can be helpful to a beginner and necessary for an old pro. And, if you have one favorite suit, there's never the problem of "What am I going to wear?"

TOPS

Above your socks or sweatpants, a tee shirt is *de rigeur*. Yes, even in colder weather a tee shirt is just the ticket under a warm sweatshirt or running suit jacket. Tee shirts of course should be loose, but not swimming on you. (Some jocks like them tight to show off their muscles, and who could blame them if they have great muscles?) The great attributes of tee shirts are: they are cotton, absorbent, often inexpensive, and interesting. You can collect tee shirt souvenirs of almost any occasion or locale—or *race*. This last is, needless to say, always impressive.

UNDERWEAR

This department should always be cotton for both men and women. Nothing should bind or chafe or cut you as you move. Bikinis with tight elastic are out of the picture. What may feel comfortable in everyday wear could rub painfully after a few miles of standard workout. Some men prefer to wear athletic supports, but many opt to do without them. William prefers the newer running shorts which have built-in supports. There are no racewalking rules about women wearing bras, but if you prefer to wear one, try the new athletic bras, and see Marion's chapter about women (Chapter 9) for details.

As with athletic supports, it's up to the individual racewalker.

Hot and Sunny

When racewalking in the summer, you'll appreciate your cotton garb, but you still may be surprised at how much you can sweat. A tee shirt and shorts is often more than enough and men may take off their tee shirts. Try to avoid racewalking during the hottest time of day (noon) and see Chapter 8 for more details. A sweatband might come in handy for keeping hair and perspiration out of your eyes; terrycloth is best. Sunglasses are necessary—prescription, if you need them—and a sun visor can be an amazing help against glare even if you're wearing sunglasses.

Hats are not as desirable as visors in the summer, as they retain heat. Some people swear by their favorite floppy, lightweight painters' caps or baseball caps, which might do if they are a light enough color to reflect heat. Just be sure nothing on your head is tight.

Use a sunscreen on any part of your skin that will be exposed to the sun for any meaningful length of time. This means the nose and face, but also might include the front and back of the knees and back of the neck. The best sunscreens contain PABA and aloe and few, if any, exotic chemical additives.

Cold Weather Savvy

The key word for cold weather dressing—something skiers and runners already know—is *layers*. No matter how cold the climate, it is impossible to racewalk in bulky coats and furry jackets. You may be surprised to find that you never need as much clothing in the cold as you think you will. But in order for this rule to work you have to keep moving. Depending on how cold things get, start with a long sleeved tee shirt or thermal undershirt (turtleneck if you prefer, as we do) and add the following:

1. thermal long underwear, ski underwear, or tights—anything to the ankle
2. one or more sweatshirts—at least one with a hood
3. sweatpants (to keep the cold from blowing up your legs because they have elastic on the ankles)
4. an extra pair of wool socks over your cotton socks
5. non-bulky sweater
6. knitted cap
7. ear muffs
8. scarf (which you can wrap around your face too)
9. ski mask
10. a nylon shell jacket—particularly if wind chill is a consideration
11. leg warmers
12. gloves
13. mittens or wool socks on your hands
14. an insulated vest.

Nothing should be bulky. Nothing should be tight. And you will only need *all* of the above list if you're out in sub-zero degrees and it's Nanook time. And don't overlook the knitted cap. A warm hat is crucial, as it keeps heat from escaping from your body via your head. You may be amazed how the addition of a warm hat warms your whole body.

If you overdress at first, don't worry about it. You can always take off an outer layer, tie the sleeves around your waist and keep on going. Of course you can't do this with the vest, but you can with whatever's underneath that.

People's tolerance to cold is an individual matter. We've seen people in the depth of winter wearing shorts in the snow, something we don't recommend because we believe in keeping the muscles warm enough to stay pliable and avoid spasm. This is why legwarmers are worn in dance and exercise classes, even indoors. As you racewalk through the seasons, you'll discover your own most comfortable way of dressing. And remember, the minute you get home, take off all wet, sweaty, or damp clothing and get into something dry and warm *toute suite!*

Rain

Rain needn't stop you from going out and race-walking. Of course we don't recommend going out in a monsoon, or a hurricane, or even a thunderstorm. But most people won't be harmed by a light rain if they dress for it, take off their wet clothes right afterward, take a hot shower, and change into dry clothes.

We have learned that wool keeps you warmest when you are wet because it doesn't soak through as quickly as other fabrics. This means wool socks instead of cotton on cool, rainy days, and wool sweaters instead of sweatshirts. As dearly as we love our sweatshirts (or "sweats," as the pros call them), we do not love the sloggy, flapping, pendulous globs our beloved shirts turn into when they get wet and weigh us down, turning our finest pace into a plodding crawl.

A sun visor is a good trick for keeping the rain out of your eyes; it acts like a little portable umbrella. Try to get the transparent plastic kind.

You might be glad to have a waterproof shell jacket—or, if you've got the bucks, a Gore-Tex running suit—or even a poncho (but ponchos don't work well when it's windy; you could turn into a sailboat). Under all of this, shorts are best for rain because your legs are waterproof.

Whatever you do for rain, let's face it, your feet are going to get wet. So grin and bear it, and take your shoes right off the instant you come home. Whatever you do, *don't* let your shoes dry anywhere near a radiator or source

of heat. Instead, stuff them full of crumpled newspaper to keep their shape and keep them from shriveling up into munchkin slippers.

Shoe Guidelines

As we said earlier, there aren't any shoes designed specifically for the racewalker yet, but we suspect the day is fast approaching. Meanwhile, running shoes are the best we have available to us. Our needs are slightly different from those of a runner, so careful attention should be paid when shopping for a new pair.

Running shoes have become a very complicated field, but we will try to keep this simple:

1. Always shop for shoes while wearing the same athletic socks you will wear when you racewalk.
2. Size can be misleading. Go by fit and feel, not numbers. For example, Marion wears a size six shoe, but needs a size eight in a certain brand running shoe; in other brands, a size seven. You never know.
3. A good running shoe has a built-up heel (1/2" to 1") and this is especially important for racewalking. Before you even try the shoe on, you can test this feature by pressing the heel of your hand on the inside heel of the shoe against a firm surface such as the floor. If the shoe heel feels too spongy and gives too easily against your hand, this shoe is probably not for a racewalker. Look instead for a firm, built-up heel with just of bit of resilience.
4. The bottom part of the heel that touches the ground should be fairly wide. For racewalkers, this is essential because each step lands on the heel. Three inches is about right.
5. The sole of the shoe should be flexible. You can test this by holding the shoe in both hands and bending it—it should bend easily. This flexibility is needed for easy pushoff.
6. The inside of the shoe should be as smooth as possible to avoid blisters.

Sneakers are not appropriate for racewalking, certainly not past your first or second day. The correct shoe will be your main or only expense. Do not let a salesperson pressure you in any way. Remember, designer labels can be meaningless. One of our favorite pairs of shoes has "Made in Taiwan" for a designer. As exhausting as the prospect might seem (and it could be more tiring than a four-mile workout), try on as many shoes as possible in the store and take your time walking around in each one. A good shoe can make or break your racewalking enjoyment, so shop with care.

Appurtenances

A wonderful assortment of paraphernalia has recently burst upon the consumer scene for the convenience of athletes: key or money holders that attach to your shoes or wrists or other parts. In fact, we have just purchased *headbands* with pockets for coins. Most of these things are waterproof, most are designed with velcro fasteners, most stay in place as they should, and most are convenient.

In the past, athletes had to pin a dollar bill inside their sweats for emergencies and leave their keys under the doormat. If they needed small change for a phone call or public restroom in the park they were often out of luck. Now you can tuck anything from a Kleenex to a credit card somewhere on your person and away you go, prepared for any emergency. Our only suggestion is to experiment with your new device for a while, to make sure that whatever you put in it does not fall out or off—do this before you use it for anything of consequence.

Watches with a second hand are an important adjunct for the serious racewalker. (See our training Chapter 5 for timing your pulse rate, checking your aerobic progress, and timing your distances.) Make sure your watch is lightweight.

Note that the *plastic* wrist bands on some digital models can trap perspiration and cause

a peculiar odor—an indication, in our opinion, of a condition that can't be too good for your wrist. You might have to change your watchband to a more porous material—and, of course, never wear the band tight on your wrist.

Other

No, you can't carry a shopping bag when you racewalk, or a shoulder bag, pocketbook, or purse. If, however, you absolutely must carry a book, towel, clean shirt, lunch, or whatever across town and you plan to racewalk to your destination, a lightweight backpack is a possibility. A bouncing jogger might find this impractical.

"Walkman" type personal stereos (Marion prefers to call these non-sexist *walkpersons*) have proven to be pleasant and diverting, but also dangerous for runners who played them too loudly to hear approaching traffic. We like racewalking out in nature and we enjoy the sounds of leaves, surf, or country quiet, but we also have had to buck distressing city clamor. These machines can also be amazingly helpful tools for memorizing lines (for performing).

A small walkperson can be worn on a loose belt or in a sweatshirt pocket, but even then the slight bouncing around will take some getting used to. They are not for serious training. They are not to be worn in the rain. And never *never* play them loudly enough to block out all sound around you. They should provide soft accompaniment and nothing more.

In Summary

Whatever you choose to wear when you race walk will be, in a sense, your partner on a very private and special—and frequent—journey So everything from shoes to headband shoul be super-comfortable to the point of feeling almost part of you. Whatever you buy for this purpose would do well to be subjected to a personal stress test: bounce around, crouch, swing your arms and legs, wiggle and jiggle and jump. You may find that all you need is what you've already had in your closet all along!

CHAPTER 8

MAPPING YOUR COURSE

Where

You'd be surprised how many ideal racewalking places exist. All the world's your track and field once you know what to look for.

SURFACE

Pay attention to the consistency of what's directly under your feet. Flat and firm surfaces are best; but they should have a little "give." Dirt, wood, grass, and cinders are better than cement. Gravel is the worst. Pebbles, rocks, and holes can be a menace anywhere. A hilly course is great for long distance runners in serious training but for people who, like us, admittedly just want to enjoy their two to five miles, a smooth flat surface is preferable. A general rule-of-foot is to go slowly and also carefully check out any new terrain.

Pay attention to what goes under your feet. The authors' favorite—a wooden boardwalk.

LOCALES

City streets

Perhaps it's the modern urban drivers' mentality, but many runners seem to head for the roads as if they thought that they were still in their cars. We find this rather strange. After all, they left their cars for health reasons in the first place, didn't they? Since (in a city especially) pollution is all around us, you don't have to go looking for it. Besides, traffic is dangerous. If you feel you absolutely must traverse a busy thoroughfare, go against the traffic and avoid rush hours when carbon monoxide fumes are at their worst.

But we think that with a little ingenuity there are other options for racewalkers. There's the old going-around-the-block ploy. (One city block is equal to approximately 1/20 of a mile, so you could go around a block 20 or 40 or more times—just try to pick an attractive block.) Usually every city has athletic tracks, school playground areas, walkways, park paths, municipal reservoirs, and zoo or museum grounds. You might not have noticed them if you never had to seek them out. Often runners who are smart enough to stay out of traffic have already sought out these hidden scenic delights, so follow a likely looking runner or use you own powers of exploration. You could well discover a whole new city within your city.

COUNTRY

The countryside is so full of racewalking opportunities, we don't even have to make suggestions, do we? If you live in the country or have access to it, lucky you!

Country roadways are usually safer than city streets, but do stay on the outside shoulders, especially at sharp turns around which can speed the one car of the day.

Moments of grandeur often unexpectedly reveal themselves out in the "wilds" with a maj-

esty and power that we believe formed the basis of much of human philosophy and religion. How much better it is to experience such moments firsthand rather than through books and pictures.

One late afternoon in early spring we were racewalking along an open expanse with the setting sun suspended in front of us—a giant red globe. At the same time, the rising full moon came up behind us—a giant silver globe! The two hung on the horizon in precise opposition for one magical instant. We probably would have missed this experience had we not been racewalking. We also cherish more modest events such as the sight of little cottontail rabbits standing as still as Beatrix Potter watercolors as we pass by. Once we were accompanied along a leaf-dappled lane by a large tortoise, who turned his wrinkled head to watch us as we outdistanced him. We have passed clumps of fragrant wildflowers in summer; gnarled, old bare trees in winter; fiery fall foliage, and groves of pink dogwoods in spring.

COURSES OF ACTION

Many city parks provide a *loop* type course: You run the same path continuously. All other types are *out and back:* You start and finish your walk at the same point. Many people try to give their *out and back* sojourns some variety by altering their return route, usually by taking a parallel path. Others are creatures of habit, and simply about face, retracing their steps.

This brings us to the penultimate lap:

THE INDOOR TRACK

Before some of you start moaning and groaning, "the tedium!"—or start having high school track nightmares—we have a few *good* things to say about indoor tracks. But first the bad news: The main drawback is that most indoor track surfaces are *angled* or *banked*, which makes racewalking rather awkward for those working on their form. It's like trying to race-walk with one foot on the curb and the other in the road. One could very well develop foot placement problems: for example, overcompensating for the track's slant with a bent ankle. Over a period of time this might be carried on to a flat surface outdoors. If you do racewalk on an indoor track often, at least go in different directions on alternating days.

The advantages of most indoor tracks are:

- No excuses in inclement weather! You can work out in cozy warmth during a blizzard—or in air-conditioned splendor while the sun is blazing.
- The social benefits.
- The other facilities such as showers, steam and sauna rooms, pools, and weight-lifting equipment.
- For those in training who are precision-minded, indoor laps are clearly marked so there's no mistaking whether you've gone 220 or 440.

WHEN: (TIMING)

It's helpful to know the times of day or night most comfortable and productive for your workout. Take the rest of your schedule into consideration. You'd probably do well to experiment to find your best racewalking times.

LARKS AND OWLS

The body "wakes up" on its own schedule, and this has nothing to do with your eyes being open or your feet being out of bed. Some people simply move better at certain times than others.

A lark wakes up at the crack of dawn and starts singing. An owl snoozes all day, wakes up at dusk, hoots, and flies through the night. Human birds are not much different. People who favor bright-eyed morning activity claim it "wakes them up." Our friend Ellen flies out

of bed, unruffles her feathers, and racewalks her way through the nearby park—without breakfast! We find this incredible. We tend to be owls: After breakfast, lunch, and much of our day's work, we're ready to roll. During most of the year, this usually means spectacular sunsets; in winter, we enjoy racewalking under the moon.

We all have days when pep seems to have deserted us—but even if you are not at your best and feeling neither lark- nor owl-like, at least give yourself a two-minute gift: start a warmup. Just start moving. Two minutes of movement indoors might lead to five minutes outdoors. Even if you can't do much more than that, it's still seven minutes more than nothing. And who knows what vast distances this might lead to?

FULL STOMACHS VS. EMPTY STOMACHS

A good rule for all activity is, don't go out right after a heavy meal. How to define a heavy meal? Anything that takes more than five minutes to chew and swallow, and probably isn't yogurt. In fact, one should wait at least two hours until racewalking after such a meal. We usually wait a half hour to an hour after eating half a light sandwich (such as cheese) or a bran muffin. But some people can't tolerate even this much before they go out. Water or other liquids are usually recommended before a long workout, especially in the heat, but some people react with indigestion, bloating, or cramps. We believe that each person should experiment—with care—when following these basic rules, to find one's own most satisfactory regimen.

(Note: Of course, go to the bathroom just before a workout.)

HEAT AND COLD

The ideal temperature range for racewalking (and almost any activity) is 40 to 60 degrees F.

But when the air goes much below or above this, cold weather, surprisingly, is a bit safer to go out in than hot weather. People tend to be more cautious in cold weather than on an inviting hot, sunny day.

You can enjoy racewalking in both extremes, hot or cold, as long as you use your brains as well as your body. People who are not used to spending time in the great outdoors may be unaware of the potential problems Mother Nature can present. Racewalking is such a pleasure that you may feel tempted to continue it even in inclement weather. If you are not a seasoned outdoorsman or outdoorswoman, however, you will need to learn to adjust to the rigors of nature. *Racewalking itself does not cause these problems,* but *any* active time spent outdoors requires a special awareness.

IN HOT WEATHER

In hot weather the most common problems—even with experienced athletes—are heat stroke, dehydration, and heat exhaustion. Overweight people are particularly susceptible to hot weather problems. Of course, all of these problems require immediate medical attention.

HEAT STROKE

The person stops sweating, the skin turns hot and *dry*, and appears reddened—all the symptoms of a high fever. There may be possible loss of consciousness.

The treatment: The person must be cooled off immediately. Get him/her into the shade and never cover him/her with anything. Pour liquids on the skin (anything you can find). Rubbing with ice is best. Rub and massage the skin to get the cooled blood circulating. The person may not be able to drink, so concentrate on cooling him/her off.

HEAT EXHAUSTION

This is the most common problem for most athletes. Heat exhaustion occurs when the circulatory system is overworked trying to cool the body. The brain becomes deprived of blood, and the person gets dizzy and can faint. The body's temperature stays normal, but the skin may feel cool and damp.

The treatment for heat exhaustion is to lie down immediately with the feet elevated, and drink liquids. The victim might feel that he/she has recovered quickly because blood has returned to the brain. The determined athlete might even want to continue exercise. Don't do it!

DEHYDRATION

Dehydration means water loss, commonly caused by excessive perspiration, and is often accompanied by mineral and electrolyte loss as well.

Some athletes claim you can prevent dehydration by drinking at least one glass of fluids before a workout and replenishing frequently along the way. In marathons, helpful samaritans are standing by along the way; but on your own private racewalks, especially during hard training, arrange to have a friend along the way or be sure to pass a fountain or drink stand. You also might want to throw some water on and over your head.

Replacing liquids immediately at the end of a long, hot racewalk is a must. The new activity drinks have been designed to supply minerals and electrolytes while preventing bloating. As mentioned in our nutrition chapter, tomato juice and some fruit juices supply potassium, a helpful supplement to water.

Excessive fat consumption is believed by some to increase the possibility of dehydration, and overly sugared drinks supposedly hinder liquid replacement. (But the well-nourished racewalker will avoid a diet heavy in fats and sugars anyway.)

Always have liquids available in summer. Plan them along your route either by passing water fountains or helpful friends—or carry them yourself. Some people have adapted plastic baby bottles equipped with a straw, and now there are soft canteens on the market that keep liquids cool as well.

HEART ATTACKS

Remember, any strenuous activity in hot weather is considered potentially dangerous to *some* people. This is one of the main reasons why a complete medical checkup is recommended.

IN COLD WEATHER

In cold weather, during exercise, the body temperature can drop. The body needs to do extra work to fight the cold as well as to keep you going. This loss of heat can lower your resistance. Most people are not aware that they sweat in cold weather. When you do, you can lose water and your clothes can get damp and chilled, making it even more difficult for the body to retain its own heat. This is one reason why overdressing for the cold can be dangerous.

WIND

Wind makes the cold worse. This is what the "wind chill factor" means. Try to start out racewalking *into* the wind, cruel as this may sound. You won't have to work as hard on your way back. It's safer not to have to challenge a gale after you've been out for a while.

Remember the old Irish proverb, "May you have the wind at your back"? Well, even though only one of us is Irish, we both wish this for you. In fact, if it's a severe wind, we wish it not to even be at your back; we wish it to be outside your house, with you *inside,* snug, warm, and sensible.

ICE AND SNOW

Do *not* racewalk on ice. A light layer of snow is fine. A deep snow can get into your socks and shoes, and wet feet plus cold is *not* a healthy combination. Ice-covered snow or thinly disguised sheets of ice are also to be avoided.

In cold weather, the most common problems—even for experienced athletes—are hypothermia, frostbite, and "cold-burn."

HYPOTHERMIA

Hypothermia means "a sub-normal temperature of the body." It occurs in cold, in heat, or in body shock; but it's most frequent in cold weather. Hypothermia is very serious at best and fatal at worst.

In hypothermia, the body temperature falls below 95 degrees F. Symptoms are slurred speech and bluish coloring around the lips, tips of the fingers, the nose and mouth. The person may appear dazed, confused or disoriented.

In the earliest stages of hypothermia the person may claim to feel fine, just "tired"—but this is not ordinary fatigue. Convince him/her to stop activity (racewalking) immediately because hypothermia can get much worse very quickly.

In cold weather, the way to deal with hypothermia is to get medical help immediately, and while you're waiting, get the person warm. Going inside is a must. A warm bath or electric blankets are also good. If you're really stuck, other people can cover the person with their own bodily warmth, preferably under a blanket.

FROSTBITE AND "COLD-BURN"

Frostbite is a danger that accompanies hypothermia in cold weather. The body will tend to sacrifice its circulation to the extremities in order to keep the vital organs at normal temperatures for as long as possible.

Unless you get hypothermia, you probably won't get deep frostbite (the kind that hospitalizes people). But what anyone can encounter out in the severe cold is a less serious type of freezing of poorly protected areas such as the face, nose, fingers, toes, and ears. What this freezing does to the skin can cause a burn-like condition complete with peeling several days later. We call this "cold-burn."

Do not rub the afflicted area, but warm it gently. Warm water immersion is good. Also, check your ears and nose, etc., while you're going along in the cold to be sure they are not getting numb. If so, return to the indoors! Areas afflicted by *deep frostbite* turn white and numb, and require professional medical attention.

TO SUM UP

Avoid noonday sun, monsoons, slippery surfaces, lightning storms, attack dogs, bicyclists, wild bulls, rampant poison ivy, blizzards, muggers, pollution fumes, and Dracula.

Remember, racewalking is not meant to be a challenge to the hazards of the universe.

CHAPTER 9

THE WOMAN RACEWALKER

BY MARION WEINSTEIN

Fashion

The ideal image of female beauty is changing and this reflects social change. Once the popular ideal was provocative helplessness, now it is one of health and strength. The accent is no longer on what's titillating for men—but what's comfortable for women. We owe a vote of thanks to our running and jogging sisters for paving the way to create social acceptability for women to appear in public while wearing running gear: shorts and tee shirts in summer and warm climates, running suites and sweatshirts in colder weather. And running shoes are now acceptable with almost any outfit, almost anywhere. In large cities it's not unusual to see women in fashionable dresses and skirts walking to work in running shoes, either carrying their higher heeled shoes in their attaché cases or keeping them at the office.

Many women categorically refuse to wear high heels for most occasions once they have experienced the relief, comfort, and increased energy derived from wearing running shoes. They wear either genuine running shoes or the latest fashionable approximations virtually all the time.

The popular feminine ideal of a thin, model-type leg is actually an unhealthy, underdeveloped, and weak leg. Dancers and women athletes have been perjoratively dubbed "too muscular" when in reality they are strong, healthy and, yes, *normal*.

This is not the place to go into the feminist political connotations of a culture which establishes as a role model the image of a woman who is thin, undernourished, weak, muscularly undeveloped, wearing unwieldy and uncomfortable high heels. But such an image has not too much to do with independence.

Racewalking has unique value for women because it is the only easily available sport that strengthens and consequently beautifies the *entire* body! Liberated or not, who wouldn't want round, well-developed arms and a firm, uplifted bustline? Since racewalking uses the upper arms and muscles surrounding the breasts, you literally exercise these with each step you take.

If you want to increase the effectiveness of your workout on your upper body, you can try carrying one pound dumbbells (pardon the expression). You can increase the weights if you wish, but we feel that one pound is adequate, because it is light enough to allow a free, unimpeded swing of the arms while adding something extra to increase upper body, arm, and breast development.

As with any bust development exercise—such as the currently fashionable weight train-

The woman racewalker.

ing ones—the miracle is that the same exercises are used to develop a smaller bust *and* to whittle down a larger bust and make it look smaller. This is because breast size is not as important as *condition*. The muscles surrounding the breast determine apparent size. The largest breasts in the world are unattractive if they hang down and graze your knees, and the smallest buds in town look great if they stand up at attention, perfectly formed, bursting with health and loveliness. This is all determined by the muscles involved, and racewalking deniably strengthens and maximizes these magical muscles.

Cellulite, Flab, and Overweight

I doubt that the writers of the Declaration of Independence had this in mind, but women and men are not created equal as far as fat and muscle distribution are concerned. Of course there are exceptions to every rule: I have several lean and lithe women friends who do not exercise much, who eat like gourmands, and who still show sleek, muscular, *hard* limbs in bathing suits and sleeveless cocktail dresses. Many of us, on the other hand—yes, myself included—hit about voting age and suddenly began to develop all sorts of unnecessary dimpling and wiggling flesh around arms, legs, stomach, and thighs. And with each year—with each *month*—it got worse! Never mind that in Rubens' time we would have been considered beauties. Rubens is not around now, asking us to pose in the buff.

There is a very good reason for these differences. Women are actually built with more fat and less muscle than men. Muscle is "metabolically active," which means that muscle is the part of our bodies that burns up calories. When we don't exercise and consequently don't use our muscles enough, we can appear

flabby no matter how much we starve ourselves, not matter how thin we become.

Cellulite is just a fancy name for fat. It goes away when we activate those parts of our bodies where the cellulite has chosen to sit. (It usually hangs out where we don't move much; who ever saw cellulite on wrists or ankles?) For women, fat, flab, cellulite, and all the other avoirdupois that the great seventeenth-century painter Rubens adored, is usually located the area from knees to breasts, including upper arms. Racewalking moves all those parts! It doesn't take a scientist to figure out what that means . . . *more* muscle, ergo, *less* fat, ipso facto: *Goodbye* cellulite, flab, et al.[1]

Changing Perspective

If you have neber been athletically inclined, racewalking may cause a revolution in your life. Any woman who remembers the hit songs of the '50s and early '60s *as performed by the original artists* has probably been taught not to move too much. Girls were segregated from boys' sports from an early age, and if they were lucky, got to play softball instead of actual basebaal, with "girls' rules" instead of regular rules. They were unquestioningly excluded from most other athletic activities, which remained for boys only. There existed a pervasive attitude in this culture that girls shouldn't exert themselves, grow muscles, look or act masculine, be tomboys, dress too sporty, or—heaven forbid—*sweat*. We were even taught to call it *perspiration*.

Many women need a new mind-set to get used to the idea of claiming their own health and vitality, just as the boys did in those formative years. The influence of culture is often so subtle, subliminal, and pervasive, you may not be aware of the extent you've been affected by

[1] Be sure to see the nutrition chapter re: complex carbohydrates for diet (pp. 45).

it. The joy is: The more alien that regular outdoor exercise seems to you, the more dramatic will be your transformation—not only physically, but in your confidence, energy, and what is, in hip jargon, referred to today as "attitude." Your outlook on life and on yourself will be different: stronger, more secure, and more pleased with yourself . . . the world will be your oyster.

An Interview With A Woman Racewalker

One such personal transformation took place in the life of Susan Friess Goldman, who became a dedicated racewalker three years ago. As she tells it:

"I was at a period of change in my life in terms of my work, and in terms of whether I was continuing with a doctorate. I wasn't working regularly. I was trying to study regularly. I was alone and without personal attachments, even though I craved a relationship; and had put on a great deal of weight. So it was definitely a good time in my life to find something, and any one thing that could have improved any one factor in my life was welcome.

"As it turned out, racewalking improved many areas for me. The first time I went out racewalking I went about, well, almost two miles. And then I went home and fell asleep for an hour and a half! That first session took me at least a half hour. I remember it was in the middle of the summer and very hot, and I just couldn't believe I was moving briskly.

"I couldn't resist getting involled with an ongoing sport, one that I could actually incorporate into my life.

"You see, there is much more in men's activities to build up the upper body and the upper arms, something not found in women's exercises. For example, I got involved in aerobic dancing, which had four or five warmup

exercises for legs, compared to one for arms. The only specific exercise that could possibly be considered an upper body exercise I think is pushups. And that's hard or even impossible for many women. So for women racewalking is a more complete exercise.

"It may be true that the pelvic area in racewalking is a more comfortable female movement, one that women can develop more easily than men. I don't know whether or not women really are more comfortable than men in this, but it seems to feel more natural to us. It's not difficult. One reason why women might be more interested in racewalking now—especially since there are more people involved— is that there are more women who are *successful* at it. It's not a purely male sport where we would have to buck a tide of men.

"The question may be more: Why are men interested in it? So much about it seems to go against things that men are comfortable with. To start, you have to assume what some people might consider a very funny looking stance. Also, men are not as lithe with their bodies, and aren't able to separate hip movement from the rest of the body. And in this sport, you must have that flexibility of thinking 'hips.' So many men can't dance because they just aren't comfortable enough with their bodies; they seem more locked in the pelvic area.

"Another good thing about racewalking—a wonderful benefit—is the weight I lost. It took me about a month before I really lost that first chunk of weight, even though I lost three or four pounds the first week I went out. This I know was due to the excess water that finally left my system. And then there was no weight change for a while, which drove me crazy because everything else was changing. My arms were getting very tight and fit, my pants and shirts were loose, and everything in my body was changing. I was getting more muscular. Things that had once fit well were now swimming on me. But there wasn't any change on the scale until suddenly: a six-pound drop! Then it became two pounds a week for a long time. I started leveling off about November after having lost 20 pounds. I realize now that when muscle replaces fat you don't necessarily see it on the scales right away because muscle can actually weigh more than fat, but it *looks better!*

"In those days I was out every day. I had restricted my food tremendously; finally, I had all the psychological self support I needed. I now had something else—racewalking—to give the cutback in food some meaning. Also, I'm lucky because I like summer-type foods: vegctables, salads, and light foods. So it all came together for me at a good time. Because I was able to feel full by having very big salads, which have very few calories, I was able to have a dramatic cutback in calories. Not necessarily in *food*, but in calories. And of course I spent those six days a week exercising. I've noticed that other women lose weight when they start racewalking, too, once the exercise becomes regular. I've seen this with women who aren't even planning to lose weight.

"But this isn't the only reason women turn to racewalking. I think running, for many women, is a very uncomfortable activity. I was uncomfortable at it; I could go barely a quarter of a mile because my knees started bothering me. And being a larger-breasted woman, I was very uncomfortable running because my breasts bounced and really hurt, no matter how secure my bra was. I think that any woman who is not very small-breasted would have a certain amount of *awareness*, if not actual discomfort, in the breast area while running.

"Besides the comfort and of course the weight loss, there's the incredible toning quality in racewalking for women. The areas that are affected most on the body in racewalking are the upper legs, thighs, hips, and the upper arms. These are the first areas where muscles start developing and the fat gets transposed. So

it's perfect—*perfect*—for women. The same areas are affected in men as well, but there are more men who are built with a more narrow hip girth than women, and the change doesn't show up as quickly. Also, it isn't necessarily something that a man is concerned about. I mean, how many men are looking to take weight from their hips? And how many women are unequally overweight? It's always the hips and thighs we're trying to reduce, and the upper arms. This is almost a universal problem, and racewalking can really help."

Finding Time for Racewalking

One of the main things that impressed me about Susan Friess Goldman was her dedication to a personal exercise schedule. When she began, she was free to work out every day, but later on she began working full time and still managed to racewalk regularly, even to the point of training regularly for races.

For many women, the idea of taking a certain amount of time out of a busy day to exercise may feel revolutionary. But try to do it daily or almost daily. Get a woman friend to go with you if you can (of course, there's nothing wrong with a male companion either) and try to stick to a consistent time of day. This will make it easier to get out.

If you are a busy mother or working woman this may seem difficult at first, but a little careful planning can pay off. Try to think of it as a job—your own personal part-time job that pays you not in money but in health, and that you must attend to, if not every day, then minimum of four times a week for the requisite distance you have chosen to go. Include in each allotted session time for warmup and warm down, and, if you prefer, a shower afterward and time to change clothes.

You will find yourself becoming quite cr

ative in snatching time during the day to get your part-time job accomplished, even if it means investing in a baby sitter for an hour or perhaps arranging barter with another woman with time to watch the children. However you work it out, give this gift of time to yourself. Your mind and body will thank you—and all those justifiable, culturally induced tensions that women were prey to back in the '50s and the '60s (for which all too often women were prescribed tranquilizers) will just be race-walked away—far away.

Unique Challenges

Too often in this culture some naturally occurring physiological functions in women are still looked upon as obstacles to an effective exercise regimen. But enlightened body-conciousness shows us it's all a matter of perception. Surely the challenges unique to women are no more horrific than the physical challenges faced by men. Believe me, ladies, we can handle it all—from bras to menopause to a masher-on-the-run!

Premenstrual Symptoms

Premenstrual tension has just been accorded enough recognition in our culture to be awarded its own initials, and now is commonly referred to as PMT. New initials or not, we've known about it for a long time—that bloated, irritable, jumpy, and possibly depressed feeling that comes just before one's period. This feeling could apear from two days to almost two weeks before, depending on your body chemistry, metabolism, the weather, or even phases of the moon. For many women, menstruation itself is a relief, cramps and all, compared to the frustration of premenstrual aches and blues.

The facts tell us that our hormones are hopping this time, and added discomfort is caused by water retention. This may or may not show up as weight gain.

One invaluable natural remedy is exercise. And guess what kind of exercise I recommend? I can personally attest to blessed relief due to racewalking at this time, although I admit my pace is slowed down, my breasts require a larger athletic bra, my armpits ache, and I have been known to sing the blues when I leave the house. But after a mile or two I feel great.

Menstruation

If you come to racewalking from running, you might know that running can aggravate cramps because of the up-and-down pounding motion on the uterus. Racewalking gently massages the reproductive organs, so it may make you feel better. But if any kind of physical activity when being visited by your monthly menses is anathema to you, you might want to cut down a bit, slow down your pace, perhaps go only a mile, or even—this is allowed, too—take a day or two off. Why not? Unless you're really in training for a race.

Pregnancy

Racewalking is safer during pregnancy than running and many other activities, but this is too important an issue to decide without your doctor's approval. Obstetricians and gynecologists are going through a revolution of their own, thanks to the women's movement (and its encouragement for women's movement), and they're learning that activity is not only OK for pregnant moms-to-be, but often may be better for them than too much sitting around. We suggest that you demonstrate a few steps of racewalking to your doctor if he or she's never heard about the sport, to show what parts it involves (and then maybe he/she will take it up also). And after childbirth, few activities are better than racewalking for getting you back into shape because of the gentle yet strengthening and effective workout it gives the abdominal muscles.

Incontinence

This disturbing problem has kept many women from athletic activities. It can be a result of muscles stretched in childbirth, and may be solved with a minor operation by an appropriate specialist. You can wear any popular brand of disposable *diapers* tucked into one or two pairs of cotton pants, and just forget about the incontinence problem; get out there and enjoy.

Menopause and after . . .

New studies are beginning to point out that maybe—just perhaps, and this is really no big surprise, is it?—the discomforts of menopause might not be a "natural" occurrence at all, but a stress-related reaction to a most *unnatural* cultural situation, i.e., the position of older women in our culture. Those women who are productive, respected by others and themselves, well-nourished, physically active and fit, rarely if ever feel any different during or after menopause than they did during the years when they were menstruating.

So now many inactive, sedentary, menopausal women are being categorically advised by their doctors to "go out and exercise." There is another, more specific reason for this: menopause diminishes the body's supply of estrogen, a natural hormone. Estrogen is believed to keep the arteries from hardening, and in men hardening arteries are linked to heart disease. So the medical equation is: post-menopausal women can be as susceptible as men to heart disease. Exercise for both women and men—aerobic exercise, moderate exercise, regular exercise—is a powerful antidote to this possible danger.

Racewalking is an ideal exercise for the older woman, specifically for one who is new to athletics. If you want to ski, run, or hurl the discus, I applaud you. But you might want to racewalk because it's easier and, in my opinion, more fun. Many older women have discovered our sport and have taken to it avidly. Mayme Bdera took up racewalking in her 60 and became a world class champion at the age of 68. An 89-year-old woman racewalker ha been seen regularly on the Central Park track. These women and many others are provin that cultural roles and clichés are not only ridiculous but outdated; and that a healthy, vibrant older woman is not only as attractive a a nubile, younger woman—she can be eve more beautiful.

Menstrual Irregularity

There is an increasingly common conditio among women running marathons known amenorrhea, or temporary cessation of men struation. Some things to be aware of are: 1) is usually perfectly harmless; 2) it does n decrease fertility; 3) it is shared with numero other women athletes and dancers, mainly ba let dancers; and 4) many non-sports doctors not understand it. If this becomes more wid spread among women racewalkers (which very well may as more women racewalke take up marathon distances), I suggest you re Joan Ullyot's (she's a doctor and marathon ru ner) excellent chapter on this harmless sy drome, a badge of marathoning for some women—in her book, *Running Free*.[1]

Bras

Certain male doctors caused quite a furor in the runner's world, when women started taking to the roads and tracks in hordes, by claiming that running "destroys" the pectoral muscles surrounding the breasts, and makes the breasts (horrors) *sag*. Some said that running braless causes the most damage, while others said that even bras don't help! I don't know about running, but I know racewalking is great for firming breasts. As far as I know, bras are not *necessary* for racewalking, but if you are used to one or prefer to wear one, try a sports or athletic bra. Make sure it's cotton, non-binding and non-chafing, without seams to irritate you, and make sure you can breathe fully and easily when wearing it. So many new kinds are appearing on the market, and because each woman's needs are different, it's impossible to recommend any brand here. I suggest that you step into the fitting room, try on the new bra and racewalk in place, swinging your arms fully to see how the bra in question feels. In the long run (in the long racewalk), the best way to know which athletic bra is best for you is to try it out. If you are a bra wearer, you may find that you like it so much compared to the feeling of an "ordinary" bra that you might decide to wear one everyday. I did.

Leotards are also comfortable and new designs offer slight support for the breasts. If you decide not to wear a bra, enjoy the freedom you feel, but remember for longer distances you may need to put vaseline on your nipples to prevent chafing against even the softest cotton tee shirt.

_____

This book contains other helpful information for women athletes and women with medical problems related to sports. Joan Ullyot, M.D., *Running Free: A Guide For Women Runners and their Friends* (New York: A Perigee Book. 1980).

Another note on underwear: Wear only cotton underpants to absorb perspiration and prevent chafing. This holds true even in winter when you still can perspire under your layers of clothing.

Social Graces

What to do when a rude chauvinist calls out to you as you're racewalking? This is not so different from the problems faced by women runners, but the unusualness of the racewalker's gait may add fuel to the chauvinist's cause. You have several choices: One is to proceed along and ignore the cad. The other is to employ an acting exercise I developed, called "more athletic than thou." Use the "actor's adjustment" that provides the strength to your inner conviction out of which you can act with realism. You must *believe* the adjustment. A good adjustment method would be, "I am training for the Olympics," and a possible expression of this adjustment would be to wave athletically in a jock-like, matter-of-fact manner and say, "How ya' doin'?" and keep going. If the chauvinist happens to be a runner, you might want to sort of salute him and say "Way ta' go!" and keep going. People won't tease you if you don't act teased. There's no payoff for them if you don't respond the way they want you to do, and they'll soon give up. Try to racewalk in well-populated areas, because unfortunately any athletic endeavor may not be safe for lone women in dark or deserted locales. Stay on running trails, tracks, or other areas frequented by runners, and go out at a time when other runners or racewalkers are out. The best course of action is always to racewalk with a friend, male or female. (Remember, the racewalker's pace is best accomplished at a rate where you can easily converse. This adds to the fun.)

Apparel, Attire, and Related Loveliness

Women racewalkers shouldn't dress much differently from men racewalkers. Comfort is the key: shorts and tee shirts in the summer; sweatshirts, sweat pants, or running suits in colder weather; hats when you need them (see Chapter 7). An added touch in colder weather is to wear leotards on your legs under shorts or on top and under a tee shirt for a glamorous version of long undies that you can let show as you go along.

It's vital in any weather, but especially in the cold, to protect your skin with a moisturizer. A light moisturizer is adequate for most women, especially since your face perspires and you don't want to clog your pores. In harsh sunlight wear a sunscreen with aloe and PABA in it—and as with anything you put on your face, as well as into your mouth, try to seek out natural products whenever possible. You may or may not be a lipstick wearer, but out in the elements, wear some sort of moisturizer or gloss on your lips.

As for other makeup, this is not recommended during racewalking; it could smear and look weird and clog your pores. Sometimes in the middle of a busy day, you may find that you have to racewalk with full warpaint—as I have—and that's fine if you must. But the whole purpose of makeup is to give you a healthy glow and as a racewalker you may soon find that makeup is redundant. In general, light makeup is best, no matter what you're up to; stay away from foundation, except the very lightest (if you absolutely must) and use the lightest blusher, too (by "lightest" I am referring to texture here, not to shade or coloring). What I have often done was to take some cleanser or moisturizer and tissue off the unnecessary stuff that I might have "had" to wear earlier in the day (for a TV appearance or whatever) and then go out and racewalk, replacing the makeup later at night when I "needed" it again. Use a good cleanser (try to match it to your skin type) at the end of a racewalking day to remove all dust and grime from your face, even if you wear no makeup at all. You'd be amazed at the soot that can collect on your face—not only in the middle of a city, but also on a country road, especially with cars passing by.

Jewelry can only get in the way. Some women are used to looking a certain way in their daily lives, but the height of fashion in an office building is not appropriate a few blocks away when you're racewalking after work or during a lunch break. Button or post earrings are fine, or tiny hoops—but anything that is heavy or dangles can spell inconvenience and/or sore earlobes. Small chain bracelets or necklaces are inconspicuous and lightweight, but heavy bracelets or necklaces can be uncomfortable and slow you down. *Light* is the key word for the weight of all accessories for the racewalker.

At the time of this writing, half of all racewalkers in the world are women. Unfortunately, just like pro baseball, basketball, and football, the Olympic racewalking events so far are for men only. Short sprint races are more available mainly for women. There are more professional opportunities for women racewalkers in international competition than in many other sports, but it seems that very few women racewalkers take advantage of this. Racewalking for women is a wide open field. If you are politically inclined you might want to change a few things, like the Olympics! In any case, whether for competition or recreation, enjoy racewalking. Remember the motto of the first suffragettes: *Failure is impossible.*

CHAPTER 10

BREAKING NEW GROUND

The difference between racewalking and running: "It's like the difference between a ball bouncing and an egg rolling. If the egg bounces, it breaks."

—HENRY LASKAU, FORMER
RUNNER, CHAMPION
RACEWALKER

Runners Convert

You might be one of the numerous runners who turned to racewalking to *improve your running*. Racewalking provides an excellent way to shave time off your running time; to work out parts of your body which you might feel running neglects (or partially neglects), such as chest, arms and stomach muscles; and to help you refine your form. It also helps with ankle and foot placement. Most runners find that the improved form they derive from racewalking workouts can then be translated into faster motion for running.

But let's face it, many runners convert.

Shin splints, tendonitis, "runner's knee," sciatica, slipped discs, low back pains ... to many, this list of potential running injuries is all too familiar. Most books on running have special chapters devoted to injuries—not only how to avoid them, but what to do about the unavoidable ones. In fact, whole books have been devoted to runner's injuries. In racewalking, the risk of injury is dramatically less.

Many injured runners turned to racewalking

Breaking new ground.

to keep them in shape until they recovered enough to go back to running. Any sport that's safe enough to perform (and perform *well*; we are talking about generous, genuine training workouts here, not merely physical therapy) while injured, has got to be safer when you're healthy, too.

And racewalking *feels* better than running. It's smoother, more flowing. There is no pounding of the head, neck, spine, and legs. Running puts approximately ten times the normal pressure on joints and ligaments, while correct racewalking can be even gentler than ordinary walking.

Running has certain benefits, but you can get identical benefits from racewalking: aerobic fitness, the pleasure of going outside regularly, improved body strength, improved posture, strengthened muscles, improved breathing, a better lifestyle, cardiovascular fitness, and heightened self-image.

Many runners feel the need for at least a few extra exercises to balance the workout their bodies get from running. In running the neglected areas are primarily the stomach muscles and the upper body, including the upper arms. In racewalking, these parts move right along with the rest of you and develop at the same pace as your legs. Many runners are drawn to the old big-frog-in-a-small-pond theory. Racewalkers are still so few that the sport provides a wide open field for new champions. You can be a star. Racewalking has races to be walked, records to be broken, Olympics to be entered, history to be made . . . . So, runners, when you try racewalking, better watch out! You might like it. Or love it. And go on to fame and fortune in the process. And we want to be the first to say, *we told you so*.

The Eye of the Beholder

Λ little over a decade ago, few sights seemed more bizarre and laughable than a runner or jogger going through the streets. Now, they are considered moving parts of the landscape; they are taken for granted, and often admired. Today's racewalkers may find themselves in a similar position to those early runners. Anyone at the forefront of a new movement (physical or mental) has had to bear at least a few gibes and/or jeers from the uncomprehending bystanders—and has borne these comments as badges of courage. Perhaps the first simians to stand on two legs instead of four were considered the odd champions of a strange new sport. Perhaps coming down from the trees in the first place was considered downright eccentric by our arboreal ancestors.

Of course the joys of racewalking might be enough to sustain you through any dreary encounters, or you might be fortunate enough to live in a community of genuine athletes. Real athletes do not laugh at racewalkers; they understand and respect our sport. However, after speaking to many pioneer racewalkers, we have found that virtually all potential problems are dispelled by following these guidelines:

1. Project a positive image, which will give you an unassailable air of confidence.

2. Keep your sense of humor, and remember th people watching you now just might end u racewalking themselves in the future.

3. Travel in groups—at least a "group" of two o more. You'll not only feel less vulnerable, you' look like a team.

4. Try wearing a tee shirt that represents somethin athletic—of course a racewalking event or clu is best. The racewalking giants we know realiz that they're advertising racewalking whenev they work out, so they wear these shirts excl sively.

5. Try the "more athletic than thou" approach. / you pass someone, just salute offhandedly ar say "How ya' doin'," or some other pleasant at letic retort.

6. Concentrate on your inner reality. The joy ye experience during the racewalking process w project to others *automatically*.

7. Remember that you are now a leader, breaking ground for other people. And finally, remember the racewalker's credo:

"A good racewalker has three essential ingredients: (1) the grace and control of a dancer; (2) the strength and agility of a gymnast; and (3) the endurance and perserverance of a marathon runner. In light of this, no one involved in the sport of racewalking should ever feel inferior to other athletes."[4]

Social Benefits

Whenever you embark on a new venture, enter a new arena, you'll find that a lot of people who are similarly interested somehow come your way. Racewalkers tend to flock together because they know they're in a minority and that fact cements ties almost automatically. Finding someone else who racewalks creates a firm footing (so to speak) for a genuine friendship. Multiply this, and you'll find you can become part of something big. And because racewalking is a recently rediscovered sport, you'll encounter many people whose growth parallels your own as you learn and progress together. This, too, is a firm foundation for sharing.

Racewalkers are friendly, gregarious people by nature. The obvious reason is that when you racewalk you can talk. In fact, you *should* talk. And racewalkers are social in the sense that there already exists a delightful tradition: breakfasting together after a racewalk in the morning. This is something you morning racewalkers might plan for and look forward to—an early morning workout with your partners and afterwards a breakfast in the grand old racewalking tradition, and good conversation about the upcoming day's activities. Or,

if you favor an early evening workout, plan on dinner afterward.

Even if you are a solitary racewalker, it's a good idea to find other racewalkers, or a racewalking club, or a coach to occasionally check your form. If you have a friend learning right along with you, you can help your friend's form and he/she can do the same for you. Even if neither of you have mastered correct form yet, you can still learn by watching each other. If you and your friend are in parallel stages of development, you can share a sense of achievement and growth as you go along, each encouraging the other and adding an additional mile together. Whenever you do something along with other people, it is a learning experience in itself. Whenever an athletic experience—a sense of going beyond yourself—is shared, there is a genuine sense of communion.

Clubs

A racewalking club provides a good chance for you to reach out and teach other people, let other people into your new world. For example, Metropolitan Racewalkers—the group we know—has no rules; you don't have to approach them at a certain time, you don't have to be an expert, you don't have to know anyone special. All you have to do is know a little bit about racewalking, and you're welcome to join.

If you form your own club, you can make your own membership rules. But the basic ideas are to share the racewalking time together, to help one another with form, to have breakfast or an enjoyable meal together, and to spread the "word."

People like to form clubs anyway. From consciousness-raising groups for women ... to men playing poker ... to book-reading clubs and theater-going clubs ... the list is endless. Well, the racewalking ideal is a perfect reason to start a club, because there's always a need for one. The whole community will benefit,

---

Martin Rudow, *Racewalking* (Mountain View, California: World Publications, 1975).

You may find yourself in company. . . .

and this is a chance for you to be at the forefront, at the very beginning of a wonderful new social wave and athletic trend.

Of course, there are clubs already in existence: The Road Runners Club, for example, exists in many cities—or you can contact your local AAU. Even if any of these or similar clubs are for runners only, they might be open to the idea of starting a racewalking chapter, and probably some of the members might want to try racewalking once they hear about it.

Once you're part of a racewalking club, you can stretch that experience further by contacting other racewalking clubs: You'll actually start to find a racewalking network. If you get serious about this and you want to participate in various races in other cities or even other countries, you just might want to travel around and meet other racewalkers. Racewalking competitions are worldwide, and still include people of various ages, abilities, and mileage. You also may find the so-called "handicap races" which enable people of different abilities and speeds to compete together fairly.

Even if you stay at home, other racewalkers can come to you. The Metropolitan Racewalkers have regular meetings at which they invite someone to speak. Your group, for example, can invite a sports doctor, a racewalker from another town, or a well-known coach to help all of you with your racewalking form and to share new information. Sweden has almost a million racewalkers. The United States has only several thousand, but the number is growing. *Your* club can help the sport grow.

As a social sport, racewalking can literally change your life. We know of two racewalkers, Susan Friess and Richard Goldman, who literally racewalked into a happy marriage. They met in Howard Jacobson's racewalking clinic in Central Park, married, and founded the Metropolitan Racewalkers. This group provides a supportive social atmosphere for regular race-walking workouts, and now sponsors an annual race in the New York area.

The Racewalking Personality

Is there a distinct racewalking personality? We're not sure, but we have made several observations which we can share:

• Acceptance

Perhaps because there are still so few racewalkers, and because it is still a unique sport, you will find that other racewalkers tend to embrace you with open arms. Few well-trained runners will probably want to run with somebody who is just starting to jog, especially if said runner doesn't know you. And what really good tennis player would want to play with a lesser one? We know many well-trained racewalkers, however, who *invite* newcomers into their club and out to racewalk with them. This may have something to do with the inherent style of the sport. Maybe racewalkers will always tend to be more democratic than other athletes, perhaps because racewalking is more involved with endurance and form, rather than speed . . . and endurance can be shared.

• Humor

Whether people who are drawn to racewalking have a sense of humor, or racewalking itself helps to *develop* a sense of humor, we are not sure. But racewalking definitely encourages one's own personal sense of joy and fun. You simply take things less seriously as you perambulate along. This is especially recommended for comedians and jokewriters, but it's an enriching side-effect for ordinary citizens as well.

• No Pain

When Marion started running, whenever she met a runner the talk inevitably drifted around to injuries. That scared her off from seriously committing herself to running. This is not what seasoned racewalkers talk about. Injuries do not seem to be part of their consciousness at all. They don't accept getting hurt as inevitable.

• Sexuality

When you are out there using your body in a very basic way, looking your best, feeling your best, and knowing you're getting even better, that's attractive. Let's face it: Good health and its pursuit is always sexually attractive.

• Individuality

This is the most exciting time (except for maybe the turn of the past century) to become a racewalker. It may be thrilling in the future, too, when perhaps the whole world may turn to racewalking, but this is a most wonderful time because now you can share in the discovery and growth of the sport. And the individuality and tenacity of being a racewalker today extends naturally to other areas of life and endeavors. It's simply so unusual to be one at this time.

CHAPTER 11

SPIRITUAL BENEFITS

*"In my afternoon walk I would fain forget all my
morning occupations and my obligations to society . . .
I would fain return to my senses."*
—HENRY DAVID THOREAU

Walking is a time-honored occupation for philosophical reflection, rejuvenation, and refreshment of the body, mind, and spirit. Just as Thoreau relished his contemplative walks through the beauties of nature, so did the more worldly Harry Truman depend upon his famous daily constitutional to contemplate the Constitution and world problems of his day. Greta Garbo was famous for her incognito walks around town. George Burns told the world he keeps fit through his 80s by walking. James Michener, in his 70s, has admittedly walked two miles a day for most of his life. John Lennon walked regularly through Central Park and other parts of New York to relax, think, and enjoy his chosen city. Woody Allen has told how he conceived and worked out his entire Oscar-winning screenplay for *Annie Hall* during long daily walks with his collaborator, Marshall Brickman.

Perhaps walking carries with it throughout life all the exhilaration of that initial moment we each experience when as babies we took our first step. Walking is truly a primal expression of human independence.

It has been said that a silent, repetitive, rhythmic action establishes an environment in which the brain can think creatively. The activity seems to cleanse the brain of its constant daily chatter. For this reason, many doctors

Walking is a form of meditation in action.

and therapists recommend that patients suffering from stress or stress-related conditions take a long walk as part of their treatment. No matter how badly one might feel—sluggish, angry, or depressed—taking a long walk helps to disperse the negative feeling.

Walking is a form of meditation in action. In a world of cars, planes and trains, we are passing through our environment more rapidly than is natural or necessary. It's disorienting. When you walk or racewalk, you experience a reorientation with yourself in relation to the world.

You're on your own two feet, re-establishing a relationship between yourself and the ground and the space around you.

Racewalking Is a Natural Extension of Walking

We have already compared racewalking to coasting or gliding through space, swimming through air, skiing, and ice-skating. These are not meant to be overly glamorous descriptions: This is how people actually feel when they racewalk.

So if you see a beautiful landscape, now you don't have to merely observe it, you can racewalk *through* it:

> I was out every day. I just marveled at how the world looked different each time. I really saw how things passed, and how from month to month the seasons changed. The colors and light are different each day. I was amazed at what nature did. I was seeing all this happen because I was racewalking in the park every day. It was a most enriching experience.
> —Susan Friess Goldman, racewalker.

Taking an hour out of your busy day to racewalk puts you back into direct relationship with yourself, the passage of time, the seasons, and the cosmos.

Peace of Mind and Body

Concentrating on nothing but movement is a method of focusing mind energy in a meditative manner. If we withhold attention from our daily problems, from the fuzz and static of the busy mind, it is almost like taking a day's vacation—with all the benefits of going away someplace wonderful without having to leave town. A pleasant detachment develops, if you allow it to, while racewalking.

While you are detaching from your problems, you are establishing your perception of the primary mind-body relationship. Your body isn't just something your mind drags around. Your body thinks and feels for itself. This bodily perception in turn affects the mind. Through your body's sensations, the mind makes its own connections. Most people are not aware of this phenomenon. In fact, the body/mind split has been considered a major cause of many of the problems in our culture. Bringing the body and mind back into their original state of harmony is a profoundly healing act.

Body influences mind, and mind influences body in a never-ending interaction. It is upon this awareness that the "new" concept of holistic medicine is based. By training the body you are training the mind in new ways. Although repetition of physical movement can seem boring, and training for a sport can also seem boring at times, perhaps we need to touch upon that feeling of boredom in order to quiet the mind enough. A quiet mind is needed to appreciate what we're doing, the actions that we're taking, and all the experiences of the moment. Many religious and spiritual philosophies advocate living in the "now" or the present moment as a source of creative and inner-directed living.

Racewalking can help you learn to cope with what in the past you might have perceived as boredom. In today's fast-paced, media-glutted world of instant gratification, it may at first be a shock to find yourself out somewhere with no television, newspapers, magazines, or movies to look at. (True, you may choose to listen to a Walkman, but for serious racewalkers this is more than distracting; it is unwieldy.) You will notice your senses becoming keener, and more subtle sounds, sights, and scents will begin to interest you. Many who have been subjected to years of media-bombardment may find their senses have become dulled. They soon realize that there are other ways to enjoy an experience besides sitting passively and allowing contrived images to act upon them.

There are no sitcoms out in the track, field, park, or roadway; there are no commercials, no Muzak, no announcers, and no pictures other than the sights past which your feet take you. You will become reacquainted with the contents and thoughts of your own head. So you will learn not only how to cope with boredom, but to use and transcend it, which leads us to . . .

Patience and Gentleness

Racewalking develops patience—the ability to stick with your effort in a non-judgmental way—as you grow. How do you get to Carnegie Hall? "Practice, practice." Well, it's the same with racewalking, and you can practice yourself right into the Olympics, or your local equivalent, and find you've become a much more relaxed and patient person in the process.

As you learn patience, so do you learn discipline. No one but you can put your body through its paces. You may find a coach, a companion, or a club, but only you will get yourself out there at the appointed times and keep yourself going. And only you can master the form correctly and achieve speed through the application of that form.

In some sports the specter of self-judgment can get in the way of enjoyment. You may find yourself feeling critical, especially in the beginning, about your personal form, perhaps comparing yourself to some other racewalker or some abstract ideal of what you "should" be doing. We cannot tell you that these feelings won't happen—they are natural—but in racewalking they are particularly inappropriate and thoroughly unnecessary. If you catch yourself in the act of self-judgment, stop immediately! Congratulate yourself for being out there in the first place pursuing your new sport and growing fit in the process. Be gentle with yourself. When those thoughts arise, just let them waft through your brain without playing host to them. Don't let them set up shop and stay there.

From a physical standpoint, whether you are a beginner or an athlete, do not force either the form or the speed; instead *allow* your body to relax into its own form and its own speed. You will achieve the excellence you aspire to with this attitude. You can take it as far as you wish to go, which leads us to . . .

Energy

One of the effects of re-establishing mind-body harmony is the release of hidden or blocked energies. In Hatha Yoga and Tantra practices, there are ways of arousing *kundalini*, a remarkable source of energy. In Eastern mythology this is depicted as a serpent with three and a half coils residing at the base of the spine. For thousands of years, there have been conflicting discussions, studies, and theories about kundalini and how this natural life force awakens. The practice involves various techniques of how to enable the energy to rise up through the six *chakras* (centers of the body located within the spinal cord). Over the centuries, there has been much debate about whether it's possible or even desirable to do this, since some practitioners have acknowledged the potential dangers of unleashing such phenomenal energy in the human being. What does seem to be agreed upon is that the kundalini uncoils and reveals itself momentarily in the briefest of instants during meditation in yoga. These glimpses of the kundalini are described as flashes of intuition and perception, which instantly revitalize the chakras. We see this coiled-up potential energy as a metaphor for the latent energy that arises from within each one of us. The awakening of kundalini—in both its mythic form and its literal manifestation—relates directly to the life-giving energy that is available to replenish and renew us all.

William has noticed that occasionally when he is breathing easily and regularly on a two- to six-mile racewalk he enters an effortless path of energy in which he is no longer consciously moving his body; his body is moving him: "It propels me along, almost taking me with it. There is no more pushing, or trying to *do*. The energy is doing what it wants, transporting me joyfully along."

The experience is exhilarating and secure, with no sense of panic. William thinks it arises from his breathing and from relaxing into the effort. But he is not sure when to expect it and so far has been unable to make it happen. It does not seem to depend on what kind of day it's been or what kind of mood he's in. We are not talking here about the "runner's high" or what happens during the last six miles of a marathon because William's experience occurs during his short daily workouts. It appears to have nothing to do with over-exertion.

This is an example of a positive outpouring of energy. An interesting point about the way our culture views energy: When it's manifested positively, it's called energy; when it's manifested negatively, it's called neurosis, anger, or depression. But in fact these are expressions of energy, too. Everybody says they want energy, but many people may not realize that they've already got it. They just may be allowing the energy to manifest in negative ways. If you consciously choose to express this energy physically, you redirect its channel, transforming the effects of its expression from negative to positive. Once the body truly gets going, there is no room for energy to depress and anger you because it is being used to propel you along the road. You can literally feel that tight, aggressive quality letting go as you hit your stride, and this eventually frees your mind.

A Personal Philosophy

Many people speak of a religious quality about going out and traversing on foot through nature; watching the seasons change, the days grow longer and shorter, the sun and moon move through the sky. Well, we agree. We think these basics are, after all, what religion is really about.

We may live longer than our ancestors did, we may have all sorts of comforts and conveniences they missed, from dentistry to plumbing to contact lenses, but they had one big advantage over us: They had easy, daily access to—and therefore felt a part of—nature. Nature was so much a part of their lives that they did not see it as anything separate or special or unique. They knew there was One overwhelming life force: They saw and experienced evidence of It, Him, or Her all around them. They lived through the seasons on a most intimate basis; their crops and, consequently, their lives depended upon their existing in harmony with each turn of the year. In Western Europe, the roots from which most of our current civilization stem, the year was viewed as a giant wheel—and as the wheel turned, the year went from winter to spring to summer to fall and back to winter again.

When you experience nature, you begin

You see yourself as part of nature.

see how all life is linked, and you understand the interdependence of all living creatures. This is not an abstract idea; you *see* it and, consequently, see yourself as part of it. You realize that you are not alone in the universe, and in fact, that no creature is separate from any other creature in the larger scheme of things. We are all microcosms of the one giant universal macrocosm or whole—and we each have an equally powerful life force. These are common perceptions of people who include nature as an integral part of their lives.

You don't have to move to the woods and live on nuts and berries, or canoe alone across the Atlantic, or live on a farm, or backpack up Mt. Everest to get back to our mutual Source— although these are all admirable pursuits. You can return to the earth simply by going outside daily (or almost daily) on city street, park lane,

or country road, and allowing yourself to experience the sky, the air, and the life around you. Nature exists in cities, too. The only places we can lose sight of it are in air-conditioned and heated buildings.

Both of us have spent most of our lives living in New York City and we have had to racewalk along busy city streets as well as through the parks and along both rivers. We have always felt renewed by this contact with the ongoing life around us. Even through the soot we have enjoyed watching the pigeons, and between the skyscrapers we have looked up to relish the changes of light and sky. We love seeing the moon rise in the afternoon—always a surprise—and watching children play stickball on the sidewalk. And when we're in the country or at the beach, we are even more thrilled. Racewalking has given us a reason to go outdoors and be enriched by our world with joyful regularity.

A pervasive problem in modern urban life is the feeling of separation or division: man from woman, one race or religion from another, human from animal, nation from nation, human from deity. Perceiving things as divided or as opposites from one another is a function of the left side of the brain. This has become just about the norm for most people today. Another way to perceive life—and a much more ancient, harmonious and spiritual way—is to realize we are all part of one integrated Whole. This is called holistic, or wholistic perception, and is believed to come from the right side of the brain. These two ways of looking at life are not necessarily in opposition to each other. Because when you have a truly holistic approach, you *understand* the other person. You don't have to agree with an "opposite" point of view, but you understand.

We are not saying that racewalking in the open air will bring about world peace, but we're pretty sure that if world leaders racewalked together through the seasons for a few miles each day, the international scene would definitely improve. And until that day comes, each one of us can get out there and improve our personal peace. And that's nothing to sneeze at, either.

CHAPTER 12

SPORT OF THE FUTURE

A Brief History

The form of racewalking as we know it today evolved organically from the natural body movements of men walking fast in races dating from the Middle Ages in Europe. Custom decreed that footmen keep pace with their masters' carriages without actually running. Hence the prototype of the characteristic racewalk gait was born. Soon a sporting tradition emerged: pitting one nobleman's footman against another's. Bets were made by the noblemen. By the eighteenth and nineteenth centuries, these private "footmen's races" or *footraces*, organized by the upper classes and performed by the lower classes, became the most popular sport in Europe, notably in England. Eventually other servants were recruited. Betting reached such a height that spectators stood along the roadway eagerly placing their wagers as the contestants passed. Thus, coachmen, footmen, kennelmen, and other personal servants became the earliest "pros" in the sport of *pedestrianism* as it was then called (from the Latin, *pes, pedis* meaning "foot").

The early eighteenth century brought a variation to the practice of walking for sport: *Individuals* who championed the long-distance walk. Again, gambling seems to have been the primary motive. In England, a man named Powell walked from York to London and back in six days or less—several times—averaging more than 60 miles a day, and "Captain" Barclay walked 1,000 miles in approximately six consecutive weeks. Walking became part of a philosophy of health and recreation by the nineteenth century. Some of the English long-distance walkers came from other sports, notably foxhunting. Many were famed for their eccentricity and advanced age as well as their long-distance stamina. "Punitive walking" events lasted days to weeks at a time, and often took bizarre forms. One walker went from Santa Monica, California, to Istanbul, Turkey, a distance of 8,000 miles—*backwards!*

In the young American colonies the most famous long-distance walker was John Chapman or, as he is still known today, Johnny Appleseed, who planted orchards as he walked across the midwest at the turn of the nineteenth century.

Long-distance competitive walking gained some popularity in the second half of the nineteenth century, mainly in England. The English Amateur Athletics Club put on a seven-mile (11K) event in the 1860s, and also sponsored the popular "go as you please" competition in which the contestants combined running and walking. These events lasted six days and were called *wobblies* or *wobbles.*

The walkers themselves were also known as wobblies, because of the combined running/walking. History does not record whether both feet remained on the ground. Edward Payson-Weston popularized the "wobble" style, as a forerunner—or forewalker—of to-

Footrace at Bayswater, England, 1851.

day's accepted racewalking technique. Weston added to his popularity by walking backwards for part of the way. He walked vast distances for large amounts of money, was financed by millionaires, cheered on by crowds of up to 25,000 people, and kept going well beyond the age of 70. He inspired others, including at least one other septugenarian, and we consider him our primary role model. He even had a sock named after him (The Weston Heel Toe Walking Sock).

By the late 1800s, racewalking took a bizarre turn with the so-called "cruelty shows" or "six-day track events," usually indoors, complete with drunkenness, gambling, and fighting among the spectators. But the walkers themselves were superb athletes who won large sums for covering up to 530 miles. The outstanding athlete in this category was the famed George Littlewood, who walked 623 and three-quarter miles in Madison Square Garden, New York, in 1888. This feat was recently heralded in *The Advancement of Science* as ". . . about the maximum sustained output of which the human frame is capable."[1] From all of sports, this accolade went to a walker—and an early racewalker at that.

In 1904, the Englishman George Larner established what can be called the modern style of racewalking, setting a two-mile world record (13:11:4) that was unbroken for almost forty years. He also set a ten-mile record and won the Olympic gold medal twice. By this time, the sport of racewalking had become estab-

[1] Article from *The Advancement of Science*, 1966, quoted by J.A. Cuddon in *The International Dictionary of Sports and Games*, J.A. Cuddon (N.Y.: Schocken Books)—a book we recommend for excellent historical racewalking details.

lished in Europe, Australia, Canada, and the United States. By 1908 it was included in the Olympic Games. Frequent arguments over proper style prompted the formation in 1912 of the IAAF Walking Commission, whose rules, still valid today, we quote in our Chapter 4.

Racewalking showed up in the Olympics in 1924, skipped 1928, but has been reinstated since 1932. Many other racewalking events have attracted aficionados of the sport around the world, and among these races some of the most interesting are the long-distance ones. The most famous is the London-to-Brighton in England, which was held on an on-again, off-again basis starting in 1886 and became an annual event in 1919. The longest annual racewalk to be found anywhere is the Strasbourg-to-Paris, which was first held in 1926. An even longer race, the Vienna-Berlin, was begun in 1893—but this 360-mile race is now defunct.

Races of more reasonable length have included the Bradford, the Milan, the Prague-to-Pödebrady, the Roma-to-Castelgandolfo, the San Fiesto Giovanni, the Lugano Cup, and the Airolo-Chiasso Relay.

Racewalking has strongholds of popularity all over the world, but since the English are credited with starting it in the first place, many hold that the English are still the best at it. Other nations to provide top racewalkers are Czechoslovakia, France, Germany, Italy, Sweden, Switzerland, Russia (notably Latvia), Canada, and Australia. The United States is catching up!

The main centers in the United States since the 1920's have been California, New York, and Ohio.

A Present Perspective

At the time of this writing racewalking is in a state of enormous transition. Once overwhelmingly popular through the eighteenth, nine-teenth, and early twentieth centuries, it was all but forgotten through the 1940's and 1950's. Now we see a dramatic resurgence as we enter the 1980's. This resurgence has been inspired by a number of remarkable walkers, two of whom are Ron Laird and Henry Laskau.

Ron Laird

Ron Laird is considered the patron saint of modern American racewalking. He has set over 80 U.S. records at distances from 1K to 25 miles and is cited in *The Guinness Book of World Records* for his 69 national championships, the most ever won by a racewalker. An heroic figure, once elusive, he is now coaching the

Ron Laird winning the National Masters 5K Walk, 1982. (John Allen)

United States Olympic Racewalking Team and is the author of the standard textbook, *Competitive Racewalking*. He has a personal best of one hour, 28 minutes for the 20K event (only ten Americans have broken 90 minutes so far), and was a member of the U.S. Olympic Team in four different Olympics (1960, 1964, 1968, and nine years later in 1976).

Henry Laskau

If Ron Laird is the patron saint of racewalking, Henry Laskau is its spiritual father. He was the U.S. walk champion for ten years (1948 to 1957), named to the Mobile Alltime Team as the foremost American walker, and won the Gold Medal for the first Pan American Games in 1951. He grew up and became a runner in pre-World War II Berlin, and would have run for Germany in the 1936 Olympics if Jews had been permitted to compete. In 1937, during a cross-country run through a German forest, the S.S. tracked down and caught some of the Jewish athletes, but Laskau outran them. Unfortunately, he was captured some time later and sent to a concentration camp. While being transferred to another camp, he jumped off the train, and escaped through Belgium and France. He traveled to Cuba and finally reached the United States where he resumed his athletic career. He switched from running to racewalking and joined the U.S. Olympic Racewalking Teams of 1948, 1952, and 1956, also winning numerous other racewalking events. He eventually became a world-renowned racewalking judge. Now in his 60s, he racewalks regularly, teaches, and continues to inspire us all.

Henry Laskau

The Future: A New Health Paradigm

Call it a megatrend, call it a social phenomenon, call it a natural outgrowth of the "me" decade of the '70's, call it anything you will—the fact is, a large body of the population is striving for health and fitness with a dedication never seen before.

In the field of medicine, doctors are increasingly aware of their patients' desire to take a more active responsibility for their own health. People want to take care of themselves and demand more of a partnership relationship with their doctors. Many books on basic anatomy and drugs, once found only in medical schools and on doctors' shelves, are now inching up the bestseller list. Along with this mood of personal responsibility for one's own health is a clearer understanding of *preventive* medicine on the part of both doctors and lay people—the importance of diet, exercise, and fitness as a deterrant to disease. Also apparent is the ideal of wholistic or holistic health care treating the whole person, healing the mind/body split.

Already Walking

In their quest for fitness, more people than ever before are *walking*, not because they have to but because they choose to. City streets are filled with all sorts of office workers wearing running shoes along with their more business-like garb, walking to and from work. These people are not runners or athletes; walking is simply the only exercise they get. Perhaps some were advised by their doctors to "take a walk." They are valiantly attempting to battle against an urban, sedentary lifestyle.

In New York, a transportation strike introduced thousands of newcomers to running shoes and the benefits of walking in the open air. Newspapers were filled with pictures of these happy new walkers trooping over the city's bridges on their way to downtown jobs—and when the strike was over, many of them kept on walking.

If only they knew about racewalking! These ordinary walkers are *just one step away* from racewalking. They would be getting extraordinary benefits from this same niche in their lives, with just a few technical adjustments. True, they're getting some benefits, because all walking reaps some rewards: increased muscle tone, fresh air, improved circulation, perhaps even some aerobic benefits depending on their pace. But if they were racewalking, they could be getting *all* the aerobic benefits including strengthening of the heart and expansion of the cardiovascular system, as well as genuine muscle development—all the health payoffs and joys of the true sport. All they need to do is carry a few items of clothing in a backpack to change into—which is good for weight training, too—and racewalk instead of walk to work. Our personal vision of the future is full-fledged racewalkers filling the city streets with strides for health.

The Old and the Young

"She's 68 and she's incredible. She did a 40K race this year, racewalking, and they have to verify it in the national records, but it looks like Mayme Bdera set a national record, possibly a world age group record: she racewalked 40K in five hours and 28 minutes. And that was her first time at the distance!"

—Nick Bdera,
member of the U.S. National Championship Team, telling about his mother, Mayme Bdera.

Taking a look at the older part of the population: We used to go down to Florida and see lots of grandparents lying around in the sun. Now the retired population has learned that the sun isn't all that good for you, and that lying around is even worse. That same age group (growing by leaps and bounds, by the way) is now engaging in sports, riding bicycles or giant tricycles, and walking. If only they knew about racewalking! But wait a minute, some of them do.

The racewalking mystique has somehow penetrated the over-50s age group. This has been a tradition, after all. Remember the 70-year-olds (and older folks) who were "wobblies" in England at the turn of the century? Racewalking opens up a whole new segment of the population to the opportunity of becoming genuine athletes or maintaining previous athletic status. This does not mean just strolling along in a "leisure" costume. This means putting on a pro outfit and working one's body to the optimum of one's ability.

At the time of this writing, the Masters is open to men over 40 and includes those well over that age, and it now has a racewalking competition. Also, the U.S. Championship Races have a division for senior men. Unfortunately, these races do not yet include women. But the prestigious National 48K Racewalk does. And one of our favorites, Mayme

Bdera, at age 68, set the World Record in her age group: five hours and 48 seconds.

Our hope is that athletes and non-athletes alike will take to racewalking into their 50s, 60s, 70s, 80s, and 90s . . . and beyond? More than 32,000 people are now known to be over 100 years old! This number is increasing each year. By the first quarter of the next century, over half the people on this planet will be older than all the others. This means that for the first time in history over 60 percent of the world's population will be older than the other 40 percent. And all of us will be up there with that 60 percent. The point here is not that racewalking is only for older people, but that you can racewalk as long as you can walk, something that can't be said about many other sports.

And what about the very young? Some experts frown on running for young, growing bones. Even without the frown, racewalking is finding its way into the high schools' physical education programs. The Junior Olympics has a competition for young walkers, and kids love the sport. Coaches are learning that a racewalker well trained in his/her youth can become almost bionic later in speed and endurance potential. More and more current champions tell how they started racewalking in high school. The National Association of Intercollegiate Athletes (NAIA) has included walking events in its national championships, both indoor and outdoor, and many member colleges offer full track scholarships to top high school racewalkers.

And for Everyone . . .
The Injured

"Running wasn't so good for me. I hurt my knees a lot. I kept tearing my legs apart. I found that anything involving bending the knees was painful. Even regular walking. But in racewalking where you're keeping that knee locked, I found it to be very comfortable. So even though I was badly injured, I could racewalk."

—Nick Bdera, member of the U.S. National Championship Team

Racewalking provides immeasurable benefits for injured athletes. Instead of sitting around the house and falling into a characteristically depressed state about what their bodies *can't* do, instead they can enthusiastically embark on a new sport. Racewalking has been embraced by injured runners, skiers, and tennis players, to name just a few. Racewalking is more than just a safe possibility for many injured athletes; it actually provides therapeutic effects to help heal numerous injuries. Small wonder these athletes often stick with racewalking long after their injuries are gone!

Racewalking is a truly gentle sport. You don't have to be a masochist to be an accomplished racewalker. Since racewalking is gentle to your body, you can develop an aerobically effective pace and an impressive, muscle-strengthening distance and have it be pleasurable instead of painful.

The Healthy

Racewalking is particularly suited as training for athletes in other sports from skiing to football because it builds up the entire body.

Racewalking is also ideal for pregnant women, many handicapped people, children, and others who might otherwise be excluded from sports entirely. And racewalking holds great promise to fill the gap left by trendy exercise regimes which come and go like breezes on a summer's day. A quick look at health clubs, some machine and weight-training gyms, and many aerobic dance and exercise classes reveals some constant facts: They are chic, expensive, and the exercisee is depend ent on teachers whose credentials or qualifications you don't usually know. If you attempt to do such work at home alone, you might not be performing it properly, audio/video tapes and instruction books notwithstanding.

Racewalking really is do-it-yourself. You might seek out a coach to help you, but you don't need one. A friend will be able to help you master the form. And once you have the correct form, if you do the warmup and warm-down before and after, the possibility of injury is a very small possibility indeed. And racewalking is free.

Racewalking is truly a sport of the past. And it seems everything on this planet moves in cycles. Racewalking then is an idea whose time has come.

CHAPTER 13

WARMUPS AND WARMDOWNS

Here is a wide variety of warmup/warmdown stretches to supplement those we presented earlier in the book. You don't have to do them all every time you go out—a warmup should take from six to ten minutes—but do try to pick five or six that involve all areas of your body. We also recommend varying the exercises every few days. Remember to breathe deeply and evenly during each one. Since we like to do our warmups and warmdowns indoors, we will start you with floor exercises. Most of these exercises are for the lower body and spine because these are the areas that need strength and flexibility, and carry most of your weight.

A special note: When you stretch or work out one side of your body, be sure to repeat the exercise using the other side of your body. And if you stretch in one direction, be sure to stretch and then relax the body in the opposite direction.

Diagonal Stretch

Lie on your back, arms relaxed at sides.

Fan arms outward.

Your right hip rolls over to the left as your . . .

Straight left leg crosses over your right leg.

Left arm moves upward to counterbalance the leg.

Feel the diagonal stretch from the fingers all the way down to the heel.

Leading from the hip, place left leg down to original position.

Repeat on other side.

Good for: stretching and loosening both sides of the body and for heightening your awareness of the diagonal force of natural opposition found in racewalking.

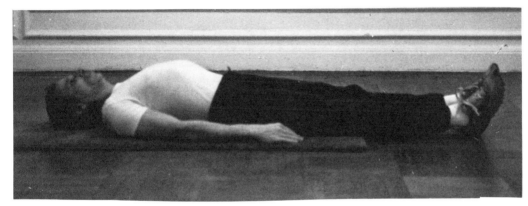

Diagonal Stretch.

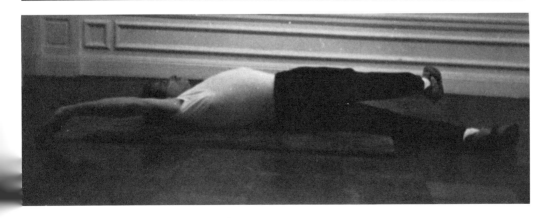

Safe Situp.

Safe Situp

Lie flat on back, knees bent.

Tighten and tilt pelvis slightly upward till it lifts off floor, the middle of spine remaining pressed to floor.

Using stomach muscles, lift head up toward your knees.

Hold for six to ten seconds.

Lower head back down and relax into floor.

Repeat three times to start, adding one time each day.

Good for: engaging the same muscles as a traditional situp—stomach, pelvis, lower back—*without overstraining.*

Easy Arch

Lie on back, knees bent.

Legs slightly apart, feet flat on floor, a foot or less from pelvis.

Tighten pelvic muscles and lift pelvis off the floor.

Feel upper part of back pushed into the floor.

Continue to lift until your back is fully arched.

Hold for six seconds.

Slowly lower from top vertebra, one vertebra at a time, and feel each one touching floor until your pelvis is down.

Do three or four repetitions.

Good for: pelvis, spine, and back of leg.

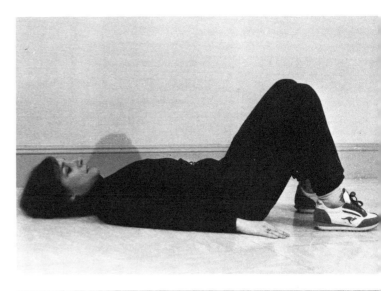

Easy Arch.

Pelvic Liftover

Lie on back, knees bent.

Legs together, lift (from hips), knees toward chest.

Let legs straighten, but not stiffly.

Allow pelvis to lift from floor, until your legs are over your head.

Lower legs over your head until toes touch floor.

Breathe deeply (from abdomen) for two or three seconds.

Optional: for even more of a stretch, allow knees to drop to your ears, encircling your head.

Good for: (not just good but fabulous) entire back, hamstrings.

Pelvic Liftover.

Side Leg Scissors

Lie on right side, one elbow and both palms on floor, legs straight and parallel, one resting on the other.

Lift left leg toward ceiling, holding toes flexed and keeping leg straight.

Lower straightened leg to starting position and repeat ten times.

Note: remember to breathe!

Good for: inner thigh muscles, and also to strengthen groin area and pelvic girdle.

Side Leg Scissors.

Pelvic Shuffle

Sit on floor, legs together and straight, toes flexed.

Extend arms loosely.

Lifting from pelvis, "walk" forward on floor moving from one buttock to the other.

Use your arms and shoulders in opposition to help you go forward.

Do ten walks forward and ten backward.

Note: don't pull yourself forward with your feet; remember to use your pelvis.

Good for: sensing and developing the pelvis and hip muscles. The swivel motion involves these muscles in an almost identical motion to racewalking.

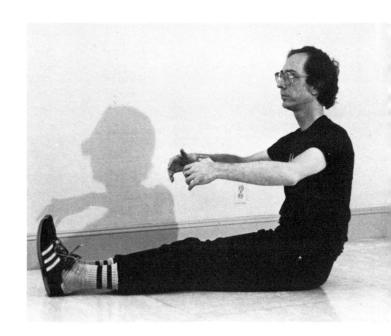

Pelvic Shuffle.

Inner Thigh Stretch

Sit on floor, soles of feet together, hands on ankles.

Pull feet as close to your body as you can.

Use elbows to push knees gently down while gripping ankles with hands.

Lift pelvis in, pulling the top of your body up and over your legs.

The top of the head moves toward ankles and away, in a rocking motion.

Good for: supple back, strengthening of adductor muscles, groin area, and pelvic girdle.

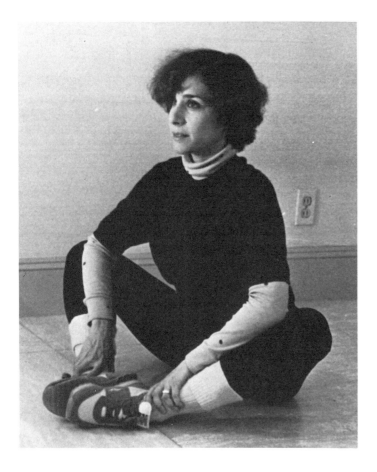

Inner Thigh Stretch.

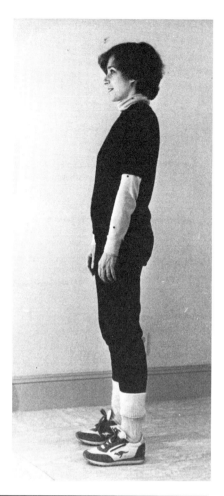

Spine Rollup/Rolldown

Stand with legs slightly apart, knees slightly bent.

Bend forward from the buttocks.

Allow torso, arms, shoulders, and head to hang to floor.

Keeping everything relaxed, hang to the count of ten.

Lift from the pelvic-groin area, slowly placing one vertebra over the other.

Shoulders remain relaxed, arms and hands hanging loose, as you gradually lift up.

As your shoulders finally straighten, neck and head are the last to rise in place.

Note: try to feel each vertebra in the neck itself as you rise.

Rolldown: Simply reverse this process, letting head drop forward first to chest.

Then let the weight of the head slowly move you back down.

Good for: balance, all-over relaxation and looseness, spinal alignment.

Leg Cross

Note: related to the spine rollup.

Stand with legs crossed with the back leg as straight as possible.

Slowly bend forward and lower vertebra by vertebra.

Try not to lift back heel.

Roll up slowly.

Good for: racewalking's straight legs and hamstring stretch.

Leg Cross.

Head Roll

Stand erect, relaxed, shoulders down.

Allow head to drop and slowly rotate the head clockwise—right, back, left, forward—in a circular motion.

Do not lift shoulders.

Note: the idea is to let some part of your head (chin, ears, back of skull) touch your chest, shoulders and back as you rotate. When you finish, think tall. (And remember, it is possible for one person to do this exercise alone. We posed in trio because we liked it so much.)

Good for: neck-vertebra-head alignment.

Head Roll.

Shoulder Roll

Stand relaxed and erect, arms at sides.

Lift shoulders up to ears.

Roll shoulders back, trying to touch the shoulder blades (scapula) to each other.

Roll shoulders down as far as possible and around toward your chest, pointing shoulders at each other.

Good for: shoulders, neck, and upper back, the racewalker's piston.

Shoulder Roll.

Leg Swings.

Leg Swings

Stand straight near a wall or other support (to be used for balance, not to lean on).

Lift left leg, relaxed and bent at knee, with right leg straight under you, arms out for balance.

Swing left leg forward and back like a pendulum (impulse should be from the pelvic-hip area). Feel how the leg arcs loosely from the hip socket.

Ten swings.

Repeat with other leg.

Good for: pelvic girdle flexibility and balance.

Five-Pointed Star

Stand erect, heels three feet apart, toes turned slightly outward.

Stretch arms up to ceiling, hands open.

Stretch right arm up from shoulder—even further.

Repeat with left arm. Feel energy with each stretch.

Six stretches, alternating arms (three with each side).

With shoulders down, bring arms out at right angles to your sides, hands still open.

Turning on left heel, move left toes 90 degrees facing outward.

Keep heels parallel.

Bring left arm straight, down to left toe.

Sighting up your right arm, turn head to look at your right thumb.

Reverse, return to center, and repeat with left side.

Note: do not twist your body. Picture yourself on a flat plane.

Remember to alternate feet as well as upper body.

Good for: perception of the diagonal, pelvic tilt, upper and sideways spinal stretch.

Five-Pointed Star.

EPILOGUE

So now you're a racewalker.
No final exams, no report cards, no diplomas—just improved health and a strong sense of accomplishment.
This may be the end of the book, but it's just the beginning of your racewalking adventures. Whether you go out for a good workout, a great time, or end up going for the gold, we hope this book has helped you on your way.
Keep at it. And hope to see you out there.

RECOMMENDED READING

Gale, Bill. *The Wonderful World of Walking.* New York: Delta Book, Dell Publishing Co., 1979.

Jacobson, Howard. *Racewalking to Fitness.* New York: Simon & Schuster, 1980.

Laird, Ron. *Competitive Racewalking.* TAF News Press, 1972.

Reeves, Steve and Peterson, James A. *Power-walking.* Indianapolis: Bobbs-Merrill Co., 1972.

Rudow, Martin. *Racewalking.* World Publications, 1975.

INDEX

clothing for rain, 53
racewalking in cold and
hot, 58–59

Weights, for training, 41–43
Weinstein, Marion, 1–3
Weston, Edward, 83–84

Women, and racewalking, 62–
70
Wool, 53